MILLIONAIRE MIND CRUSH

Discover The Inner Secrets Of Creating A Million Dollar Online Business. If You Are Going To Make Money, Make It Big

KEITH EVERETT

Copyright © 2021 by Keith Everett

All rights reserved.

No part of this book may be reproduced in any form or by any electronic or mechanical means, including information storage and retrieval systems, without written permission from the author, except for the use of brief quotations in a book review.

Under no circumstances will any blame or legal responsibility be held against the publisher, or author, for any damages, reparation, or monetary loss due to the information contained within this book. Either directly or indirectly. You are responsible for your own choices, actions, and results.

FTC Disclosure, some links in this book may be affiliate links. This means that the Author/Publisher will receive some compensation in the form of commission from the sale of the product.

Enjoy the book.

Worldwide Copyright held at Copyright House, London EC2R 8AY, England.

CONTENTS

Introduction	v
1. The Apprentice Millionaire	1
2. Fat Cats	10
3. Millionaire Mind Habits Part 1	18
4. Millionaire Mind Habits Part 2	33
5. Dark Corridors	39
6. What Makes A Millionaire?	44
7. Marshmallows And Money	52
8. Show Me The Money	59
9. The Million Dollar Business	67
10. Compound Or Die	80
11. I Have No Money, But I'm Open To Offers	84
12. Multiple Streams Of Income	93
13. Keep It simple	103
14. Advice From The Heart	109
Conclusion	113
Sources and Resources	117

INTRODUCTION

"Yesterday is not ours to recover, but tomorrow is ours to win or lose."
– Lyndon B. Johnson

I remember the day clearly. It was the day that I lost a massive $250,000. Yes, you heard that correctly, a massive $250,000 in the space of a few minutes. GONE with the click of a button.

Did it hurt?

ABSOLUTELY. The pain was extreme. I felt like I had been shot.

It's not every day that you get to experience that gut-wrenching, stomach-churning feeling of flushing $250,000 of your hard-earned cash down the toilet.

This was a life-changing experience for me, and one that I swore I would never repeat.

A few years ago I would probably have gone into a drunken stupor for days and thrown all my toys out of the pram.

But this was now.

Life was different.

I was a different person now. My mind was different. "It's only money," I thought to myself. "It's not like I've lost a leg."

My mind had expanded. I was somehow bulletproof now to bad events. I had completely outgrown my fears. I had completely bottled up sixteen cans of WHOOPASS! and somehow injected them into my brain.

I was FREE!

This event was one of those many events I had experienced in this rollercoaster journey that we call life. A Dark event that would test anyone. I was now immune. You can be bulletproof too. WHY NOT? Problems are not the actual problems that we think they are.

You are about to take a different view on all of your problems. You are about to have an epiphany. A mind switch.

Are you ready for a total mind makeover?

Had I won the Lottery? Maybe I was just so flush with cash that a "mere $250,000" flushed down the pan was only a drop in the ocean to me.

No. It wasn't lottery money. I had made that money through being an entrepreneur and some came from selling my house in 2017 before I went travelling.

It was a massive shock

I shook with rage.

Well, for a whole five minutes, at least.

I was going to buy a new house with that money. Now I was bruised, battered, and houseless too.

The pain was for real, but a headache pill was not the cure. It's all in the mindset. It's in the way we think about what's happened. Your mind can make you, or break you like a twig.

When something bad happens to you, it instantly becomes history. How you deal with that piece of history determines what happens next. This book is about to introduce you to the realms of becoming mentally INVINCIBLE.

Your mind can do strange things to you if you let it. No matter what happens to you, you can always turn it around, survive and prosper.

You can overcome anything.

Losing $250,000 in a single day was a shock, but shocks are tremors to be expected, and you defeat them when you have the best mind power in your arsenal. In this book, you will fully develop your mind to withstand any mental bomb that the world can throw at you.

This book is full of dark corridors of discovery, places where I'd rather not visit, but we all go there at some time. We can stay in the darkness or we can come into the light. We could all do with a massive shock now and again, even if it is just to jolt us into taking the action that we know we should be taking.

Look, no one likes to admit it but, we are all a little bit vulnerable. We all have many dark corridors living in our head. Mental blocks hiding within us, just waiting to be unblocked.

Take a firm hold on your life, loosen those tight knots within that keep you from achieving the very things you want.

Does it seem like you're always trying to do your best in life but you never get a break? Do you feel downhearted, overwhelmed or stuck?

This is a book about giving you the mental powers and practical advice to make a million dollars. You will do this by using the fastest way forward. Yes, you've guessed it, the Internet.

It doesn't matter if you already have a brick and mortar business, or no business at all, you can always add more value and more revenue by using the Internet to expand and explode your business.

This book will give you the mental preparation you need to get EVERYTHING you've ever wanted. That's a bold claim, but I've been doing this for over 40 years now, I know a thing or two about what it takes to make a lot of money.

We all need to upgrade our thoughts, and in order to do that, it starts here, right here with this book. This is the mental medicine that so few people have been able to get their hands on.

Let's break free.

No holds barred.

This book is like no other self-help book out there.

Just like I did in my previous book, 'Money Mind Crush', I am now asking you to fasten up your seatbelt and hold on tight.

This is going to be one hell of a ride...but first I have a free gift for you. My report "Millionaire Shortcuts" is available FREE here.

https://keitheverett.co.uk/shortcuts

About the author

Who is this guy Keith Everett?

Here's a quick story

I went from newspaper delivery boy to teenage delinquent, to serial entrepreneur. There, I told you it was a quick story.

Ok, you asked for it, here's some more. I have been a serial entrepreneur since I was 13 years of age. You name it, I've sold it. When I was a kid, if things weren't nailed down in our house, I would sell them.

I frustrated the hell out of my poor mum. She was a loving woman, but a very tough cookie, who tried to keep me in check. She would buy me stuff and a little while later, I would sell it. I didn't feel bad about it at the time because when you are a kid, you tend to only think about yourself anyway.

Back then I had a wild entrepreneurial streak in me and a constant hunger for turning things into money. I still have this mad streak today.

I've owned many, many businesses over the last 40 years or so, mostly brick and mortar type businesses but in the last ten years, they have all been digital businesses.

Digital is really where it's at in the 21st century. You seem to be able to buy and sell just about anything online these days, even cars.

I have studied all the great motivational & inspirational business speakers over the years and I've learned my craft from my experience of doing it on the battlefield, plus I've also benefitted from having some insanely good mentors.

I don't have a Ph.D. or an MBA. I just have the ability to turn donuts into dollars. I don't think there is a degree for that, but I'm happy to do that until I expire. If you are like me, you are a person who likes making money.

I like to keep my mind as SHARP as a razor. I still want to be out there kicking a*s when I'm 100 years old. There is so much garbage out there about being too old, too young, too tall, too short, etc. In my view, it's all rubbish. You are never too ANYTHING. You just have to get out there and do it.

Your body is your car, you got to this place where you are now in your life through every fault of your own. No excuses.

Do you want to know more? **I did say this was a short story**.

OK, briefly then…

I have created several digital products over the last few years and I've created the odd digital course. I currently blog a lot and I write books. My current business model is a publishing company.

I used to do everything in business myself, but this is not such a good idea if you want that elusive freedom lifestyle. I presume this is why you are here, to make a ton of money, and then to spend the rest of your life doing the things you love.

Amen to that.

I've been rich, and I've been broke. Rich is just a number that you are satisfied with. Some people consider themselves rich on $50,000 a year. In other parts of the world, you could live on $50,000 for the rest of your life.

Being rich is a hundred times better than being poor. As Michael Douglas said in the 1984 film 'Wall Street'; "There is no nobility in poverty," and he is so right.

The best way you can help the poor is to not become one.

With money, comes responsibility. You can help a lot of people if you have the money. Giving can be just as much fun as receiving.

Becoming rich increases your options. Whether that is eating better, seeing more of the world, spending more time with your loved ones, etc, etc. Or maybe you just want peace of mind. I know I do.

I will be directing you through every single step of your journey.

This is a book that will take you by the hand along the path to total financial success.

This book is split into two sections. The first section is the mental work: this is POWERFUL and absolutely KEY to your training. It's no use trying to be a tiger if you are currently thinking like a pussycat.

The second section is the practical work. But, before we do that, let's get the mental work done first. Take your time, there is a lot to learn. Don't skip through the chapters and peek at the practical work (you know you want to).

Once your mind is ready, we will then concentrate on the practical ways of making that **MAGIC** million.

1

THE APPRENTICE MILLIONAIRE

Did you ever see that wonderful movie, "Let It Ride"? If you did, do you remember this quote?

"You could be walking around lucky and not even know it." – Richard Dreyfuss.

What has luck got to do with it?

Although the film 'Let It Ride' (1989) is purely fiction, it is based on a taxi driver called Jay Trotter (Richard Dreyfuss) who has his best ever day gambling at the track.

The quote itself actually makes a lot of sense.

You never really know what you are capable of until you let the genie out of the lamp. Your idea could be the best thing since sliced bread, but unless you release it to the world, you will never know. By the way, does anyone know what was the best thing before sliced bread?

I'm joking, of course.

You exploit your 'lucky side' by going above and beyond. Taking calculated risks can, and often will, increase your chances of success.

Luck is the result of placing yourself in the right place at the right time. In other words, meeting opportunities and deliberately putting yourself in front of them.

In the case of Richard Dreyfuss's character (Trotter) in the film, it started with a conversation he overheard in his taxi between two guys about a horse that was expected to win. I think one was the trainer and one was the owner.

Dreyfuss went to the track, he backed the horse with $100 and it won. He took that as a sign that this was going to behis lucky day and he just carried on betting.

He was looking for a sign. He felt lucky. People are always looking for signs. A sign, really is that gut feeling within that this opportunity is it. It's also about your ability to feel lucky enough to 'go for it'. In other words, having the confidence to do it.

Trotter started with $100 and ended up winning half a million dollars. He just kept rolling his money over and over on each race. He finished with a massive $68,000 all-or-nothing bet at 8/1 on the final race. It won (of course), netting him a cool half a million dollars.

I'm not advocating that you should gamble. It was just a film. The actual true odds of pulling off a six or seve-horse accumulator on any given day would be astronomical.

But, it's true. You could be walking around lucky and not even know it. Especially if you don't put yourself out there. If we equate luck to our actual life, only around 5% of what happens to us is actually random. 95% of what happens to us is actually controllable by us.

What has this got to do with developing a Millionaire Mindset?

The winning mindset starts like Trotter's first bet of $100. BE BOLD. His first bet won and that gave him the confidence to have bet Number 2 and so on. You may not have the confidence to be as bold as brass at the moment but by the time you've read this book from cover to cover, you will.

Confidence.

This is what happens in real life when you start a business and you get your very first success. It gives you the confidence to attempt your second step and so on. We need to acknowledge that luck does in fact exist, but not to use it as a financial strategy. The better we get at anything, the luckier we get.

Your next idea could be your very own million-dollar idea.

Having a plan.

How do we know if our idea really works unless we are prepared to give it a shot? It's kind of weird really, but a plan of direction in life does not seem to be a priority with most people. We create plans for most things:

- We plan a holiday

- We plan what we want in the supermarket

- We plan what to have for dinner

- We plan what movie to watch at the cinema.

Yet, very few people actually plan for the future. Most people's plans for the future are left entirely to chance.

We need to start planning as early as possible. I use a journal. Each evening, I write down what I want to achieve the next day. Start doing this today, and make it a regular habit.

I use an actual pad and a pen. The act of writing it down physically seems to trigger a different response from the brain. I can remember things a whole lot better if I've written them down, rather than if I've typed the words into a word doc.

Try it.

Without a plan, you are already planning to fail. Thoughts are things, start to get your thoughts down on paper, make this a daily habit.

Writing (and reading) keeps the mind active and young. You're probably heard the old saying "leaders are readers and readers are leaders". This is very true. Reading and writing actively engages the brain, your brain needs exercise, just like your body. Constantly staring at a TV screen can start to deactivate the brain, as your brain becomes more passive watching TV.

TV is a bit like chewing gum for the eyes.

Our mind is our greatest asset.

The mind is like a muscle. The more we use it, the stronger it gets. The more we use our minds to work smarter, the more smart money we can make.

Money doesn't just appear. It dribbles into our lives in the form of a weekly or monthly pay check. In a job, I would just about earn enough to keep a house going, pay the bills, and have some left over at the end of the week to put toward a holiday or two.

I don't think we were put on this earth to just survive. I'm a firm believer we were put here to thrive.

I think of working for a boss as 'Jar Money'.

However, if we work smart and work for ourselves, we can be on 'Bucket Money' before very long. I know which I prefer. I want my money to be in buckets, rather than in jars.

In order to graduate from Jars to Buckets, we need to think bigger.

There are no truly unique ideas. There are unique ways of implementing those ideas, and that's how we need to start thinking.

Start asking yourself questions like: "How can I give great value and offer a unique way of doing it?" Most things that you see selling like crazy out there are mainly old ideas that have been given a new coat of paint.

This book is a collection of ideas. I'm not the first person to think of them, but I'm the first person to arrange them in this unique way and put them into this book.

This is how you create any product. You put together ideas in a unique way and market them. It's not rocket science. People make it much harder than it actually needs to be.

We could all, in fact, be "walking around lucky and not even know it".

As apprentice millionaires, we must stop acting as our former selves and start acting in the expectation of receiving large sums of money as our new selves.

Let's leave the past behind. Whatever your former life looked like, are you ready to start living in positive expectation?. Maybe you are already a positive thinker. Maybe you just need a few ideas and some inspiration. If that's you, let's put that 'game face' on and get ready to roll.

Expect the best and the best will appear. Expect the worst and, well, we all know how that ends.

In order to have a new role in life, you need to start to experience that new role before you actually get it. You have to imagine what that role looks and feels like.

Can you do that?

Can you see in your mind's eye how your success would look, feel, and even smell like?

That new car – can you 'touch it'? Can you 'feel it'?

A lot of people call this 'Faking it till you make it'. However, we are not faking it, we are experiencing it through our senses. What this does is warm up the subconscious mind into positive expectation.

When we convince our mind that we have already achieved our goals, we are tricking it into thinking it's already a done deal. The mind then wants more of the same, spurring you on to pursue those goals.

The reason most people don't get what they want is because they spend their lives focussing on the things they don't have. Keep telling yourself "I don't have this" and "I'm always broke" and guess what...

Your subconscious sees this as an instruction to keep you there. Your subconscious mind is monitoring you 24/7. Yes, even when you are asleep.

Things appear in our minds way before they appear in physical form.

Think of your mind as being like a huge iceberg. The bit sticking out of the sea that you can actually see is your conscious mind. This is the part of the mind most of us use the most. We tend to use this to navigate our way through life, and we try to keep away from danger.

Our subconscious mind is the most powerful part of the brain, this is the brain's thinking brain. This is the part of your mind that operates your "gut feeling", it is the part of your mind that can attract anything good to you if you would only let it.

That huge, hidden part of the iceberg underneath the sea, that is your subconscious mind. It's vast. This is the part of the mind that we use to do those extraordinary things. Master this, and you are golden.

And just in case you were wondering, this is not some woo-woo weirdness thinking, thought up by hippies from the sixties. This is simply drawing physical experiences into your life by using the power of thought, which is something we all do every day.

Stay with me here.

Let me give you an example. Imagine something sad. Now imagine something extremely sad. Your mind doesn't know that it's only imaginary. Every thought you have releases a certain chemical into the brain.

Each chemical releases a feeling.

This is how we can make ourselves physically cry just by thinking about something very sad. Maybe you were thinking about the passing of a loved one. Maybe it was the loss of a lover. The event is now over, yet our thoughts are creating a sad feeling. This feeling is now making us cry.

This is how you are tricking the brain. The brain doesn't know any better; it believes what you tell it to believe. We are recalling these events and making them 'real' again. The subconscious doesn't know if the event is true or false.

This doesn't happen when you are asleep. Your dreams are processed differently by your brain. This prevents you from being harmed if you happen to be having some kind of wild and weird dream that involves jumping off the top of a ten-story building.

How you see the world is everything.

Many people see the world as either black or white. They either think the world is a wonderful place, full of opportunities and they live in positive expectation, or they think it's a fearful, dark place; a place where you constantly have to avoid problems. Life to them is a struggle, and they are constantly trying to avoid being hurt.

The truth is, the world is neither good or bad. It is only how you perceive it. If you see it as a dark and dangerous place, it will be. If you see it as a land of opportunity, it will be.

Your outer world tends to be a reflection of your inner world and how you think about it. Our life, therefore, tends to fit the pictures that we constantly hold of it in our minds.

Right, let's move on.

Key takeaways:

- **Luck** – This is something we ourselves control. Only around 5% of what happens to us is purely random. We all have the ability to control the other 95%. Good luck really is all in our preparation to meet opportunity head on, and to grasp those opportunities with both hands when presented with them.

- **Having a plan** – We seem to have a plan for everything else, holidays, supermarket visits, days out, etc. But we have no plan in place for the most important things in our life, like our financial future. This is crazy. We can't leave everything to luck.

- **Engineering the experience in our minds** – Everything in this life started off as an idea. Someone thought about it first before it appeared in reality. Think of any building, car or experience.

It started as a thought. This is how you can start to elevate your life experiences right away. Start to feel 'lucky' and imagine yourself as a more wealthy person. See it in your mind's eye. Feel it, touch it, experience it in your mind. This is how you attract things to you in the physical world.

2
FAT CATS

"They live, we sleep, we starve, they eat. You must comply with their deceit, don't trust the wolves to guard the sheep. They'll colonize when you close your eyes into a superpower that will never die."— Trevor D. Richardson

Giving is a good idea.

"*Give and you shall receive,* your gift will return to you in full—pressed down, shaken together to make room for more, running over, and poured into your lap. The amount you give will determine the amount you get back." (**Luke 6:38**)

Luke was a pretty smart guy.

This act of giving should not only be a charitable act, but it also applies very much to a smartly run 21st century online business too.

Have you ever been out shopping in a supermarket and you come across these people handing out free food samples? These free samples are designed to whet your appetite to go and buy the product.

It's what we call a loss leader.

It's the same in the online business world. Give a sample of your product to your potential customers upfront and people will love you for your value. People tend to buy into people these days. With the power of social media, if you want people to buy from you, you need to be transparent and honest.

People are not stupid. They have a very sensitive nose for Bullsh*t, and can easily tell if you are not on the level.

Check out some of the biggest names in the personal development industry, I'm talking about people who make multi-millions per year.

Les Brown, Tony Robbins, Peter Sage, Mel Robbins, etc. What do they all have in common? They are always transparent in what they do, they give away lots of free advice before they expect you to buy anything.

Check out YouTube and you'll see plenty of videos of people giving away lots of free advice. This gets people interested enough in them to keep coming back for more and eventually buying from them.

They give, and they keep on giving.

You don't have to be a high-profile speaker to make this work for you. Most people who are making money online aren't. I'm certainly not. I hate public speaking. Give people good value up front before asking them for money, and many of those people will actually go on and buy from you.

It's the law of reciprocity.

When you keep giving, people will often feel obliged to return the favor, and they will often do that by buying your products.

When I released my first book, 'Money Mind Crush', I offered up review copies to people. Some people still actually went out and bought the book even though I had given them a review copy.

This was simply because I had given people value up front over the years from my many videos, my blogs, etc. People will give back to you if you provide a lot of value up front.

When I first heard about giving stuff away to make money, I thought it was a dumb idea. At first I couldn't see point. But after doing this a few times, I increased my revenue many times over. The difference is, we now live in the 21st century and the way that we do business now is a lot different from before.

People want more these days. Consumers are a lot more savvy, and they expect more from you. Companies don't last very long in business if they give a sloppy service and sell rubbish products.

Giving value away for free upfront creates raving fans. Those fans will keep coming back for more. You are effectively creating your own hungry crowd.

And hungry crowds will buy.

On the other side of that coin are the people of slime

Slimeballs in action.

Here's what not to do.

You've seen them, the slick, slimy, salesmen and women in action on Facebook. They friend you up, you accept, and before you know it, there is a message in your inbox that begins with "hi"

They then launch into this crazy sales pitch. "Buy my stuff, buy my stuff." It's like a horror show from the 1990s coming back to haunt us. This, in my opinion, is very poor marketing.

Sometimes, they don't even say hello before they send you their giant copy and paste sales message.

How rude.

Pitch, pitch, pitch...

This might work on the odd occasion if someone is desperate for a chat, but it will turn off far more people than it will turn on. It's not exactly a great way to start a long-term business relationship.

Think about your life partner. When you first met them, did you ask them to marry you on the first date?

Probably not.

No, you warmed them up a bit. Maybe you took them out for dinner, got to know the parents a bit before you decided to pop the question.

Maybe you were even a modern-day sinner, and you just lived together first. (no judgment here) Lol.

People need warming up.

Give people stuff for free.

This could be something as simple as a free gift to get people on to your list. It could even be giving a series of useful tips on your blog or just some free, instructional videos on YouTube.

Whatever you give them, don't ask them for money the minute you set eyes on them. Never chase money. It will just keep running.

The way to get money to come to you is to give people value up front. Money will then follow you.

People are not walking cash machines. They are human beings with feelings, they have real problems and a life. Treat people well and they will reward you with their custom.

Treat people badly and they will never be a customer. In fact, if you treat them badly, they will tell others to never be a customer of yours either. Good news travels slowly, bad news travels faster than the speed of light.

Build relationships with people. Then you'll build customers.

Fat Cats.

Have you ever seen the cartoon of the little 'Fat Cat' guy with a top hat and a cigar poking out of his mouth? He has dollar bills falling out of his pockets and he even has a chauffeur-driven Rolls Royce.

But, he is also very mean. People don't like him, they don't respect him. He never leaves a decent tip, and people loathe him.

This is, of course, a very outdated image of a rich person. Real rich people today don't go out of their way to look rich. Today's millionaires often work from home and their pinstripe suits and top hats have been replaced with jeans and a T-shirt.

It's not all about looking rich and showing the world that you are wealthy. This tends to have the opposite effect. If you continue to brag about how much you have, you turn a lot of people off, and it shows people how much of a bighead you are. People get fed up seeing people brag about their wealth.

I do believe we all have an opportunity to grow and contribute to this world. A business is a great vehicle to showcase your talents and contribute to society.

When you give people value, especially for free, you are building up a universal bank of credit. This bank will pay you back a hundredfold, not necessarily by everyone to whom you gave, but it will come back to you.

So, let's assume, you are doing all of the above things but you have yet to taste success. How long do you give it?

My answer to this is quite simple. You need to give it as long as it takes.

Don't keep quitting.

People start a perfectly good business, but often at the first sign of trouble, they give up.

This is MADNESS!

Quitting will get you nowhere. If you just keep quitting, you only get good at quitting. It's not enough to just try. You need to keep going, no matter what.

As Yoda said, "**Do or do not. There is no try**."

Sure, sometimes you have to quit the path that you are on. It doesn't make sense to continue on a path that is clearly not working out, but you should never quit on your dreams.

Everything worth having will never come to you in a straight line. Nature doesn't work like that, every river has a bend. Expect to be challenged over and over again.

Earlier on in the year, I lost $250,000. Did I give up? Of course not. It was one of those bends in the river. Every time you are challenged and you overcome that challenge, you grow a little bit more.

I have learned over the years that if you just keep going, eventually the breakthrough you want to appear will appear. Most people avoid this breakthrough because they are constantly quitting things when the going gets tough. They spend their life quitting and then starting over again.

This is crazy.

You probably won't get it right the first time. Look back in history at all the people who have done amazing things, I don't remember any of them saying they got it right on the first attempt. Thomas Edison, Colonel Sanders, Henry Ford, Fred Smith, Bill Gates, and Mark Cuban spring to mind. These entrepreneurs failed time and time again before finally getting it right.

Sometimes, the difference between success and failure can be purely down to just not giving up. When you quit, how do you know how close you were to winning?

If your goal is worth having, it's worth failing for.

If you want to be a millionaire, you have to start thinking the way a millionaire would think. These people are tough, they are focused and they are relentless. Nothing stops them.

You never know what you can do until you push yourself to do more. The human spirit is very, very powerful. It will only break if you let it.

Key takeaways:

- **Create an online business for the 21st century** – People expect a lot more nowadays. Give first before asking people to buy. By giving away samples of what you do upfront, you'll attract more followers, some of whom will become raving fans and buyers.

- **Fat Cats** – This is an outdated image of the modern day millionaire. Today's multi-millionaires are much more likely to work from home, wear jeans and a T-shirt, and give millions of dollars to worthwhile causes. They tend not to go around trying to convince people that they are rich.

- **Don't keep quitting** – You can't get to where you want to go if you become a professional quitter. It takes time and possibly many failures to get to the level of financial abundance that you want.

3
MILLIONAIRE MIND HABITS
PART 1

"*Our happiness depends on the habit of mind we cultivate.*"
– *Norman Vincent Peale*

Developing Laser Beam Focus

Millionaires are not superhuman. However, they do think differently from your average person, not because they are any better – they aren't – but because they think better.

Most people are spending a great amount of their entire lives just trying to get by. This is understandable, as we all have to find enough money to pay bills. Life can be tough, very tough at times.

The quality of our life is affected greatly by the way we think. It's only when we elevate our thinking that we can truly sample a better standard of living. No one owes us anything. **WE owe us everything**.

Our brain uses up approximately 20% of all our energy. This is an amazing power-packed computer that we have living in our heads. It's a terrible shame to not make greater use of it.

We are so much more powerful than we give ourselves credit for.

In this chapter, we will be working on each of the powerful mind habits that make up the millionaire mentality.

The first habit we need to concentrate on is focus (no pun intended).

My advice here is to not chase two rabbits at once. You'll end up losing both of them. Work on one thing at a time. As a man, I know we are not that good at multitasking. We can just about sit on the toilet and read the newspaper.

It is so easy to chase shiny objects. They glitter like gold and tempt us with their quick ways to wealth and riches. I've looked at shiny objects on the Internet over the last 20 years and I don't see any of these schemes still working today.

Money making schemes, investment schemes, things that look too good to be true, probably are, and will end up leaving a big hole in your bank account.

Many of these schemes tend to be of value only to the people who start them, and maybe a very few early adopters. The majority of these schemes crash and burn, taking people's money with them.

The first thing we really need to do in order to develop focus is to get rid of all the distractions around us. Find some quiet space.

Get rid of distractions.

Designate an area in your home or office as a place that you won't be disturbed. Make it clear to your partner, your kiddos, and the family dog that this is to be a no-interruption zone.

Even if you have to clear out the garden shed or garage, get yourself some quiet space.

Turn off your smartphone, steal yourself away from Facebook and other social media distractions. Designate a set time each day for some uninterrupted work time.

If you are working a full-time job, maybe you can spare an hour or two in the evening after you have had a meal and spent some quality time with your partner and kids.

Give everyone in your family the amount of attention you can all happily live with, and then go to your quiet place to work your two-hour slot, or whatever time you can find.

Get yourself a timer to time your work sessions. An alarm clock works fine, or use one of the many online timers available for your computer. Just Google 'Online Timer' and you'll get plenty of options.

Set your timer for however much time you have. If you have two hours, then set it for two hours, and get started on your first daily task. Don't get up from your seat unless you have either finished the task or you need a comfort break.

Focus 100% on the job at hand.

Get used to using longer periods of sustained focus. You are training yourself to be a master of focus. This will require a lot of discipline from you.

Just by doing this one thing, has enabled me to write complete books very quickly. I now create an entire book in half the time I used to take. I've doubled my productivity since mastering this technique.

My very first book took me nearly a year to write because I got so distracted. I would write a bit, put it down, go do something else, come back to it later, write a bit more.

No wonder it took so long. What are you yourself doing now that could have been done in half the time?

Keep this focused time period going daily. Practice this each and every day, and I promise you, you will become at least 100% more productive than you were before.

Develop this skill, and with practice and you will have achieved something that 99% of the population doesn't have: bulletproof focus.

Concentrate on one element of your plan at a time, use one time period to complete one task. If you finish the task in the time allocated, congratulate yourself and then set yourself another task to be completed in another fixed time period.

This is simple, but very effective.

Let's move on to our second millionaire mind habit that is absolutely essential to master:

Being Decisive.

Dynamic Decision-Making

Believe it or not, decision-making is just like any muscle. The more you use it, the better you get at doing it.

In business, you need to always have your finger on the button. You need to be OK with making decisions quickly. You will be making decisions about what to sell, where and when to sell, how much you need to charge, etc.

You will also have to be making decisions to put things right when they inevitably go wrong.

Business, like life itself, is similar to navigating a series of hurdles. You tend to get over one and then you get another staring you in the face.

Make decisions quickly, change your mind slowly.

Being able to think quickly and think on our feet is something we all need to cultivate. We can't keep sitting on the fence when it comes to decision making because nothing will get done unless a decision is made.

You might say that sitting on the fence is a decision in itself, but who wants to spend their life sitting on the fence?

Decisions are everything.

Where you are in your life at this very moment is the outcome of all of your decisions and habits that you have made up to now, good or bad.

This is why decision-making is so important. Being decisive is one of the top mental keys to success in anything that you may ever undertake.

People respect decision-makers. It makes them stand out as leaders as so many people are bad at making decisions.

Step 1. Don't Overanalyze.

When you are about to make a decision, it's always good to have the information handy. However, don't use that information to overanalyze everything.

Get used to making a decision quickly by asking yourself these questions:

A) If I do this and I get it wrong, what is the worst thing that can happen?

B) If I don't do this, what will it end up costing me?

This might sound like a simple formula, which it is, but I've used this for years, and it works.

Human beings do tend to overcomplicate things. It's almost as if everything has to come with an instruction manual in order for it to be validated. The truth is, most things in life are simple until human beings get a hold of them.

Start to see your decisions as the rungs on a ladder. The better you get at making decisions, the smoother the journey up the ladder it will be for you. If you can't make a decision in a short period of time, let it go.

What is a short period of time?

In business, you want to be making decisions in minutes, not hours or days. Obviously, if it's a huge business deal that could make or break you, you will want to give it more time to weigh up all the options, but most decisions can be made in seconds.

Step 2. Overcome Fear.

In decision-making, stop fearing the worst. Some people never make a decision because they are so frightened that they may be wrong. I've got news for you. In business, as with all aspects of life, you will be wrong many times. The only people who never make a mistake are those people who do nothing at all.

Don't fear being wrong; embrace it, it's a learning curve. The more decisions you make, the more accurate your decisions will eventually become.

Step 3. Make Smaller Decisions More Often.

If you haven't been very good at making decisions up until now, don't beat yourself up over it. Many people struggle with decision-making. The best way to get over this is by starting with making smaller decisions, but get used to making them fast.

All of us make decisions every day without thinking about it. From the time we get up in the morning, to deciding what to wear or what to eat, we are constantly making decisions.

It's time to SUPERCHARGE the process.

Start making decisions that you DON'T normally make every day.

This will start to rewire your brain into thinking differently. Most of the everyday decisions we make are on auto-pilot. Start giving your brain something a bit more lively to think about.

Most people give their bodies a workout. Now, it's your brain's turn. It's no good giving your brain 20% of all your energy but never asking it to do anything. It's like having a personal computer on your head but never turning it on.

You are in charge, so get it working.

Build up slowly. Decision-making should be fun, not an ordeal. Practice making those small decisions each and every day, then slowly raise the game. Switch it up, make slightly bigger decisions, then BOOM! Before you know it, making big decisions will become the norm.

This will be life-changing.

Keep feeding that decision-making muscle in your brain until you are a decision-making NINJA!

How To Develop Bulletproof Resilience

Resilience - the capacity to recover quickly from difficulties

Before we get fully into the power of resilience, I want to emphasize just how important this quality is.

We all get knocked down, some more than others. Sometimes, the most terrible things happen; loved ones die, perhaps we were the victim of a horrible attack, etc. I want to say right here, right now, how you cope with what you went through, is everything.

Most bad things that happen to us can be turned around and hopefully learned from. Erasing memories, especially painful ones is hard, I know that, but it can be done.

Here is a quick story from me. This is one of those dark corridors I was talking about earlier.

The Day I Lost $250,000.

I will cut straight to the chase here. We are all guilty of doing stupid things. None of us are perfect and if we were that perfect, think just how boring life would be.

I suffer from occasional stupidity just like anyone else. No matter how much knowledge you acquire, you will always be prone to making mistakes and doing stupid things. After all, we are all flawed human beings.

This is one of those stupid mistakes that I can laugh at now, but at the time, the pain was real.

It's our failures, our mistakes, and how we deal with them that define who we are. I used to be the person who wouldn't admit that he was ever wrong. Instead, I would search and search for evidence that I was right.

When you accept your flaws, relinquish yourself of your past mistakes and wipe the slate clean in your mind, you automatically free yourself up from carrying any emotional baggage, and you are then able to move forward.

Living those mistakes over and over again in your head is a sure way to feel depressed and you'll end up feeling stuck. Don't wallow in your past mistakes, forgive yourself and move on.

Let it go.

My darkest hour.

I have been in some bad scrapes in my time, I've outrun the law in my teens, I've spent money like water as if I were some playboy, I've had marital problems, drink and drug problems in my teens. I've suffered from low self-esteem and I've even been driven to the brink of despair.

I've overcome a lot of things in my life.

But...

During the recent Covid pandemic, I made a huge mistake.

You could say it was the mother of all blunders. It doesn't matter how good you become at business, or how good you become at judging human nature. You will still make mistakes.

In 2017, I sold my house. I gave most of my 'stuff' away to charity, and I went traveling. I kept my laptop with me and I ran my online business from my car using Wi-Fi stops along the way, including McDonald's™.

P.S. Their Wi-Fi is very good, the coffee tastes reasonable and you can easily spend a couple of hours inside your McDonald's office undisturbed, for the price of a couple of coffees.

All was good, business was good, and the money was rolling in.

At the end of 2018, a good online friend of mine recommended an automated forex (foreign exchange, trading) deal. It was purely hands-off and for the next 18 months, all was sweet. It seemed to work well and all of us made money.

The problem was, I got lazy. I let my online business drop off as I would be sloping off down to the beach most mornings, sipping coffee and just living off the income I made from this super forex deal.

Life was good. I was bringing in around 7% profit (after fees) per month. This, of course, was a big difference from the bank's pathetic interest rates of 0.02% per year in the UK (at the time).

Also, as some banks had collapsed in the previous recession of 2008, I didn't want to have too much money floating around in them, just in case it all went belly up. As we got to March of 2020, news of the pandemic was starting to take hold.

I decided to take a substantial amount of money out of the bank that was paying virtually zero interest and I put it into this forex deal. After all, things had worked out well in the previous 18 months.

Oh boy, was this a BIG Mistake.

To cut a long story short, it all collapsed one day in April of 2021. The trades had been in a massive hedge (this is where trades are taken out in the opposite direction of the current trades, in order to stop your liabilities from getting any bigger). The problem was, the trading company who owned the bot couldn't figure out how to get us out of the mess, so one day they just decided to pull the plug.

And we all lost around 93% of our money.

I personally lost around $250,000.

Could I have done things differently? Of course. We are all wise in hindsight. If only we had that crystal ball.

Did I listen to my gut instinct?. eh, No

When things go horribly wrong, what is very important is how you react to it.

You could spend the rest of your life beating yourself up for past mistakes. Or you can let it go. All you can do is OWN the mistake, and don't do it again. Move on.

Don't walk around with past mistakes playing over and over in your head. You'll eventually drive yourself nuts. Come out of the darkness and into the light.

Mistakes, especially giant dumbass ones like this one, are just curveballs that the big boss upstairs throws at you every now and again to keep you from getting too complacent.

If life is getting a little bit too comfortable, expect a wake-up call.

I got money lazy.

They say you can't have too much money. I believe this is true, but you can have too much easy money. Money, where there is no exchange of value is not good. This is why over 60% of lottery winners are back to where they started after just a few short years.

Easy come, easy go.

Even spending money can get boring.

Just look at the demeanour of many of the idle rich. Drugs often become a vital part of their lives to alleviate all that damn boredom of spending money.

At this point, you might be saying, "That's a nice problem to have." Yes, it was, but after spending 18 months of doing near enough nothing and just having more money arrive each and every month without me doing a single thing, it bored me to tears.

We all need a purpose in life. Spending money and dossing around on the beach isn't much of a purpose.

I have to admit that the one thing most of those success books don't tell you is that if you have a lot of money coming in from all directions, you can get a little bit too complacent about things.

This is when mistakes are made.

Lesson learned.

I have a question for you.

How would you personally feel about losing $250,000?

At first, I tried to avoid everyone who knew I had invested in that forex deal. After all, when you drop a gigantic clanger, the last thing you want to hear is, "I told you so."

I did eventually speak to a very good friend of mine, who was shocked. He said, "What are you going to do now?" I thought about it for a few seconds and then I blurted out.

"I'm going to think BIGGER!"

And this really is the secret.

If you lose $250,000 like me (don't), you have to out-think the loss by reducing in your mind, the value of the loss. Does that make sense?

I'm not trying to be a wise-ass here, but just because you drop the clanger of all clangers doesn't mean life as we know it has to come to an end. The impact of the loss on you is in direct proportion to the intensity you give to it.

In other words, a loss of $250,000 could be crippling if your whole life depended on it.

SO what did I learn from all this?

- **I was thinking too small**. If I was earning that $250,000 a month, it wouldn't have come as such a huge shock to my system. I needed to up my game and think a lot bigger.

- **You can always make more money**. It wasn't like I lost an arm or a leg, which is more permanent. Money can always be replenished, even if you lose the entire lot.

- **If it sounds too good to be true, it probably is**. I should know this as it's the very thing I teach. However, I am also human and will always make mistakes in my life.

The trick is to learn from them.

I saw this as an opportunity to stop being lazy and to no longer rely on money coming in each month from some 'deal'. I needed to go back out there and get back down to the fundamentals.

And that's what I did. I created my new publishing company.

When the clanger drops, don't keep concentrating on the clanger. Too many people spend their entire lives thinking about all the things that have gone wrong, or are likely to go wrong. This is MADNESS.

Life is too short to keep giving yourself mental pain. Concentrate on your next move and how you can use your mistakes to drive you forward and move on.

It gave me a totally new perspective. If losing $250,000 makes that much of an impact on my life, then my thinking wasn't big enough.

If $250,000 was all you ever had in the world and you lost it, it could be a disaster, but if your monthly income was

$250,000, it wouldn't make too much of a hole in your finances.

The size of your thinking determines the size of your bank account.

The value of money to us is in direct proportion to the value we give it. If you view $100 as a lot of money, it will be, and if you earn $100 a day, it probably is. But if it was your hourly pay, you wouldn't be too badly affected by losing it.

By looking at money in a different way, we can overcome our resistance to seeing every dollar as such a big deal. Money goes where the bigger mindset flows. Our resistance to this fact is what keeps money away from most people.

I created a new goal in my mind. I decided to go for a massive goal of earning $250,000 a month.

When I achieve that, the loss of $250,000 will seem like a pebble in a pond (hopefully).

All problems are just opportunities in disguise.

What is the point of this life if we can't overcome the bad events that happen to us and replace them with good events? Bad events will always pop up in our lives. You can't stop that.

So, don't even try. Concentrate on creating good events instead.

We are all a long time dead. I'm sorry, but this is true. Imagine spending your whole life focusing on your bad events. Wouldn't that be a terrible waste of a life?

Step 1. Accept the past and decide to move on.

Step 2. Forget the memory, master the emotion. It's the emotion that keeps you anchored to the past. Change the way you think and feel about that memory. Introduce a new, more positive thought pattern toward it.

For example: What can I learn from this? How can I use this experience to teach others?

Step 3. Concentrate on the future. Spend each day planning your new, more positive future. Having so much to look forward to will help you erase those painful memories.

Step 4. Keep learning. Spend time each and every day improving your education. Find time to learn. This keeps the brain active and fills your head with useful, positive information. Use this information to create a brighter future.

Step 5. Don't take life or other people too seriously. I pay very little attention to criticism. You can't pay your bills with other people's opinions. Develop a bulletproof attitude towards others. Filter what you choose to accept from them, and dump the rest.

Key takeaways:

- **We talked about the need to develop laser beam focus** – Don't chase two rabbits at once or you'll end up losing both. Find a quiet space in your home or office to concentrate on one task at a time.

- **Dynamic decision-making** – Don't overanalyze things. Make small decisions at first, but make plenty of them. Develop that decision-making muscle more by using it regularly

- **How to develop bulletproof resilience** – Change the emotion you have toward the event. When things go bad, always have plenty lined up to look forward to and learn from the lessons of the past.

4
MILLIONAIRE MIND HABITS
PART 2

The Power Of Confidence. I don't pretend to be the most confident person in the world. Let's be honest; is anyone?.

True confidence comes in many shapes and forms. Not everyone is confident in absolutely everything they do.

My confidence grew out of achieving. However confident you are at present, getting nearer and nearer to your target of $1,000,000 will definitely improve it.

The weirdest things can start to happen when you get yourself out there and start to have a little success. The problem lies, when a person won't get out there, and this is nearly always a lack of confidence rearing its ugly head.

Increased confidence comes from when you realize your true worth. Many people are walking around thinking that they are just not good enough.

This is crazy. Good enough for what? and, who says so?

No one has the right to tell you whether you are good enough or not. People who continually interfere in your life and spend their time putting you down have no real place in your life anyway. Stay away from negatrons.

There are enough critics in this world. If these critics actually went out and did something useful instead of criticizing other people, the world would be a much better place.

Steps to a new, self-confident you.

Step 1. Don't connect your self-worth to your net worth. Your bank balance has nothing to do with your value as a person. We are all worthy, rich or poor. No self-made millionaire ever started out with a million. In fact, many millionaires were in minus figures before they got started.

Step 2. Don't compare yourself to others. Most of the time, when we compare ourselves to others, we are comparing apples to oranges. We are not comparing like with like.

We don't know the struggles that a person has endured. If they are in front of you today, let it go. Aim to catch up later and overtake them. The only person that you need to compare yourself to today is YOU. Are you better today than you were yesterday?

Step 3. Face your fear. I will relate this to the day I did my first to-camera video. I was petrified. "What if I mess it up? What if no one likes it?" I thought to myself, "You can either do it or keep running scared and never do it." I did it, it wasn't good, but the next one wasn't too bad, and now I've created hundreds of videos.

The more you do something, the better you become.

Things won't change unless you overcome that inner nagging doubt, silence that voice inside your head, and take the plunge. I guarantee you will thank yourself for it later.

Step 4. Be a possibility thinker. I thought of all the things that I said I couldn't do and realized I was now doing them. You are the same. There must have been things in your life that you said you couldn't do, but you did them anyway. I know I did. Don't get stuck in the moment.

If your mojo is low and you feel trapped right now, get out and do new things, meet new people. If you don't yet have that confidence, imagine what you would look like if you did have the confidence. How would you act, where would you go, how would you feel, what would it look like?

Create a brand new image of yourself. See yourself doing the very things that you originally feared. Now put those thoughts into action. Give yourself a pat on the back after each and every victory, no matter how small. And never, ever give up.

Let's get into the next mind trait that is going to blast you forward on your new journey.

The Power Of Persistence

This is a BIG one.

But first, a quote.

> "Patience, persistence, and perspiration make an unbeatable combination for success." – Napoleon Hill

Although I have included persistence last in our mind habit section, it's probably the most important millionaire mind habit that you can possess.

Why?

Because some people tend to think that any great success in life is only for the chosen few. Those people that are highly skilled and are super powerful businessmen or women

This couldn't be further from the truth. Some people spend so much time learning skills that they never end up doing anything with them. They become professional students. Getting a degree is not a guarantee of success, in fact, a lot of people never even get to use use their degree's.

I would rather have persistence than skill. Skills are fine, but persistence makes you skilful at whatever endeavour you attempt. It's almost like a battering ram to success, whoever persists, wins.

I have friends who start something, they get a few knock-backs and then quit. I have had hundreds of knock-backs in my life but I just keep going regardless, eventually, the results come.

Persistence will win in the end. I know people who have been trying to get rich for years. Some are still trying, some have quit and those that persisted have either made it or they are very close. It's almost as if the universe rewards those who are too stubborn to quit.

Speaking from experience here, most of the ventures I've succeeded in were failures at first. I don't recall any of them being easy.

Steps to developing persistence.

Step 1. Start with your why. Why do you want to do XXX? If your 'why' is big enough, you'll keep on going. Imagine the pain of not achieving your why. Perhaps you promised someone near and dear to you that one day you would all be living in a big house by the sea.

Imagine the disappointment on the faces of those around you if you didn't deliver on this. Make a pact with yourself to see things through till the end. Convince yourself that you will achieve that goal no matter what, burn the image of you achieving that goal into your mind.

Step 2. Expect things to be harder than people tell you. I have noticed that in the last few years, Internet marketing gurus who used to use terms such as, 'Easy', 'Push Button', 'Business in a Box', etc., are using these horrible marketing tactics less and less now. People are getting wise to the BS.

Anything that makes a lot of money on a consistent basis over time is not easy. It can be simple, but it's never easy.

Step 3. Model successful people. Find a role model. Aim at a target worth aiming at. If you wander around aimlessly, not knowing what to do, then you can have all the persistence in the world, but nothing good will come of it.

You must have a target.

Aim at the bullseye. Find the best people around you who are doing what you want to do and model them. Model what they do, their habits, their approach to marketing, etc. (don't copy). It's not hard to find out what they're up to and how they are doing it.

Most high-profile people have a social media presence. You can easily find out what your target person is doing and the steps that they are taking to achieve it. They either have a course that they are selling or a series of YouTube videos outlining what they do.

In this digital age, most successful people online share a lot of information about themselves, what they do, and how they do it.

Step 4. Find an accountability partner. Life is a lot better with like-minded people around. You can find accountability partners in anything you do. Someone out there is doing the very same thing you're doing, and may also want to be held accountable too.

For everything that you are trying to achieve, there are thousands of other people out there trying to do the same thing. Find out where these people hang out and approach them. A great place to find accountability partners is on Facebook. There are groups for just about any subject under the sun on there.

Join a group, friend some likely candidates and message them. They can only say no. Keep persevering and eventually, someone is bound to say yes.

Key takeaways:

- **We talked about the power of having confidence** – Don't expect to be confident in everything you do. You get more confident as you achieve more. Don't connect your self-worth to your net worth, you are more than enough, rich or poor.

- **Persistence** – With persistence, you can achieve just about anything. This is probably the most important mindset we've discussed so far. Without persistence, people give up, and sometimes they give up just a few steps from the winning line. This isn't you: you will carry on until you reach your goal.

- **Find an accountability partner** – No one is an island. It's good to be in your own business, but people make our life better. It's even better to have people around you with the same interests as you. Choose an accountability partner and stick to them like glue.

DARK CORRIDORS

We all have them. Those dark places where fear and loathing hide. I think it's only fair that if I'm writing about success, I should write about the downside too. This are my own experiences.

It's easier to fight an enemy if you know where it's hiding. Most enemies are hiding within.

Not everyone will understand what you are doing. I remember as a guy in my early twenties, how some of my friends reacted to my hunger for being in business, it affected many relationships. Let's be honest, most people want to just work a 9-5, go out, get drunk on a Friday night and relax on the weekend.

I thoroughly get that.

As an entrepreneur, it's different. Your mind is always on the game. You live it, you breathe it, no one will ever see your journey the same way that you do.

It can get lonely.

In fact, some people may see you as a possible threat to them. This is often how the human psyche works. If you are not on the same page as other people close to you, it can often lead to conflict.

If you are struggling to make ends meet, have a family, perhaps you are employed in a job that you hate, you have a huge conflict of interest. The first problem, could be your partner. They can't understand why you are 'messing' with this online business thing when you should be concentrating on just going to work and seeing the family unit survive.

You can't blame them for thinking like this. Most people just want to keep their head down and get through life without any trouble.

The next conflict is perhaps the one you may be having with yourself. We are often on a see-saw of emotions. We live, trying to keep what we have, whilst also trying to obtain more. We want certainty, but we also want change. and change brings about uncertainty.

This see-saw of emotions can affect our mental health. We can sometimes feel guilty for wanting more. After all, aren't all entrepreneurs just greedy people who think about nothing else but money?

There are some political persuasions out there who might try to convince you that this is true. However, it's not true at all. Some of the most useful and most generous people in the community can be entrepreneurs.

You and I are people who just want to squeeze the very best out of life. We know that we are only on this earth for a very limited time, we are trying to do our very best for our loved ones, so why shouldn't we GO FOR IT!

Get comfortable with being uncomfortable.

If you want more, and you clearly do, otherwise you wouldn't be reading this book, be prepared to lose a few friends along the way. It's a sad fact of life. Once you start to break out of your comfort zone, there will be all kinds of advice from all kinds of people on why you shouldn't be doing it.

This is actually a vague attempt by them to stop you from trying to outgrow them. People get fearful around those who want to change. The answer is to start seeking out people who are on the same journey as you.

As I said earlier on in this book, you don't need to get rid of your current peer group, just upgrade it to include more people who think like you.

No one needs to be around negative people. The journey you are on to completely change your life is hard enough. You will constantly be fighting demons of doubt in your head. The good thing is, the tough journey ahead is preparing you for the best that is yet to come.

Darkness is always replaced by light. Life tries to give us an even spread of challenges and good fortune. It is only us who interrupt this process with our positive or negative thinking. The more positive we think, the more positivity we attract.

Also, challenges are a bit like buses. They seem to clump together and all arrive at once. Don't be put off by this. The more darkness you overcome, the better you become as a person. Strength comes from getting over challenges.

I've been told several times in my life that I see things through rose-tinted glasses and that I have a strange way of viewing the world. My answer to criticism, and yes, some of it has come from my family, is: I see no sense in being locked in a world of negativity where people only see the darkness.

I see no sense in criticizing and blaming others for events that happen in life. I alone am responsible for things that happen.

If you want to grow, if you want unlimited success, no matter what that means to you, then you have to be bold. You can't live two lives; you can't be a wallflower, living a life of quiet desperation, someone who never wants to be seen or heard, and also be a resounding success. You have to choose between the two.

Only you have the power to give yourself the power.

There will be times when you want to give up. There will be times when you get sick and tired of trying and not getting the results you want. This is the time when you find out just how tough you really are.

When people say to you. "You'll never be any good at that," remind them of the countless people who came before you and went on to do it. When people say to you, "You can't do that," what they mean to say is, they can't do it.

I always remind people who find it appropriate to criticize me for wanting more, and wanting to be more, that if people like us didn't exist, everyone would be out there working for the government, there would be no new inventions, there would be no entrepreneurs providing jobs for people.

And finally...

Sometimes, you will feel alone. When the world is out there snoozing, you might be working, when all of your friends are down the pub or out clubbing, you might be grinding.

You are paying the price now for the huge gains you'll make later on.

The wonderful thing about working for yourself is you don't have to pay any attention to the weekend. You are not governed by set vacations and government holidays. You can relax and enjoy things as and when you want to.

Onwards and upwards.

Key takeaways:

• **Be prepared for some people to not like you** – People may even start to snub you as they may feel you are about to leave them behind. The problem lies with them, not you.

• **Be prepared for self-doubt** – This happens to all of us, even the uber-positive. Don't let it stop you, drive right through it. Be prepared to face your darkest corridors. Sometimes you will feel alone.

6

WHAT MAKES A MILLIONAIRE?

he number one reason most people don't get what they want is that they don't know what they want." – T. Harv Eker

Are entrepreneurs born or made? That's a good question. The answer to that is both. Some people are just natural entrepreneurs right out of the gate. They sell their toys and turn their comics into money.

You've seen those pictures on social media of a tiny little tot running a lemonade stand or a cute little girl scout selling boxes and boxes of cookies.

In the USA, people aspire to reach the American Dream, allowing their highest aspirations and goals to be achieved. And being an entrepreneur plays a big part in that.

Maybe these entrepreneurial kids are also heavily influenced during their early childhood by their mom or dad if they were entrepreneurs themselves.

But not everyone is. Many people grow into being entrepreneurs. Something, one day, will set them off. Maybe it is the loss of a job, or perhaps they just get fed up spending their lives working for a lousy boss.

Let's face it, jobs are useful: they serve the need for getting bills paid, but it's hardly likely you'll make a fortune being in one.

I was a young entrepreneur.

I won't bore you with all my early exploits, I just know that I had the entrepreneur bug at a very early age. It seemed a very natural thing for me to do.

You sometimes don't know what your true calling is until it hits you right in the face. You could go through life not knowing what you truly want to do then, BAM, all of a sudden you realize it.

"I really, really want to do this"

What makes a millionaire?

Well, the obvious answer here is a million dollars. But in order to produce those million dollars, you need to think a long way outside of the box.

Perhaps you know this box as your comfort zone. We all have one, but the tighter yours is, the less risk you'll take, and the less risk you'll take, the less money you'll make.

I know that you know this, but just avoiding risk is a risky strategy.

We take risks every day but don't think of them as risks. NOT being an entrepreneur is also risky. It's a bit of a risk working fifty years of your life in a job and not having enough money to live on during retirement.

This happens to millions of people all over the planet. They reach retirement and they get short changed. After living 50 years of your life on full pay, many people have to end up living on peanuts in retirement.

Personally, if that's comfort, then I'll avoid that zone.

Making a million is not as hard as it seems. It really isn't. It just looks a big number.

If you put it into perspective, it's only the equivalent of a couple of half-decent houses in this day and age. It probably wouldn't even buy you the roof of a house, if that house was situated in the suburbs of Los Angeles.

Whatever it is you're doing now, whether it's a job, a side hustle or full-time self-employment, you can do this. Make up your mind right here and now that you will make a commitment to make a million dollars and set yourself a timeline.

Set huge goals.

If you set a huge goal and you don't quite reach it, that's a lot better than setting your sights too low. If your goal is a million, set a goal of ten million. Who knows, you might make five, six, eight, or even the whole ten.

You can turn your life around in a heartbeat. It's all about thinking bigger and not settling for less. Decide NOW to approach the future with full-on positivity. Take action. Actions always have and always will speak louder than words.

What next?

Our next step in the millionaire mind cycle is to accept something quite strange, and this will probably confuse a few people.

Becoming a millionaire is not all about the money.

I know that sounds a little crazy, but becoming a millionaire is not just about the money itself. It's all about what you give, not what you get. To put it simply, you earn massive amounts of money by creating massive value.

A lot of people get this wrong. This is why a lot of entrepreneurs are not millionaires. It starts with giving. When most people set themselves up in business, they make it all about them, and they purely concentrate on taking and making.

If you keep chasing money, you'll never catch it. Let money chase you. You do that by giving first. People love value, they run after it all the time. Let it be you that they run to.

Obviously, you have to create the right business model and you need to know that what you are about to do is going to be potentially profitable. But the focus should always come down to satisfying your customer's needs and solving their problems – how can you be the one to solve them?

Once you figure this out. You are good to go.

Make it all about them. People will love you for it.

The Mastermind Group

Another way to skyrocket your mindset and your income is to be part of a mastermind group. In Napoleon Hill's book, 'Think and Grow Rich", he talks about the coordination of effort from two or more people.

Forming an alliance.

Although we see ourselves as being 'self-employed' and in business by ourselves, we have to remember the importance of being around other like-minded people.

You don't have to be in business alone. There are millions of other people out there on the same journey as you. When I started the publishing business, I joined groups of other publishers. What this does is, it gives you access to knowledge, potential partners, possibly people who provide services that you could use, and you may even end up making a few lifelong friends along the way.

I'm talking about a meeting of the minds. By leveraging other people and their ideas, we can improve ourselves greatly. In fact, as Napoleon Hill will testify, when you form an alliance with like-minded people, you are multiplying your mind-power many times.

It has often been said that you become the average of the five people that you hang around with the most. If you hang around with people who are winners in life, perhaps people who are aiming to create million-dollar companies, this will also rub off on you too.

How do you upgrade your peer group?

The best thing in my view is to first distance yourself from people who have a negative influence in your life. And then increase your circle by making friends with people who have a positive disposition.

See less of friends or relatives who don't support your vision. Few people even have a vision. You want to be around people who have a vision. Be around supportive people, especially people who are heading in the same direction as you.

If you want to meet other like-minded people, join Facebook groups where other people like you are hanging out. Make the first move, add people to your friend list who you think will be a good fit for your friends list.

I have made many good friends on Facebook, and I've actually met up with many of them.

Another good way to meet entrepreneurs is to sign up for events. I've done a fair bit of this over time. I've been to Orlando in Florida, Las Vegas in Nevada, and many, many business events all over the world.

It's an amazing way of meeting people who think like you. You get to spend days hanging out with them and getting to know them.

When you find a handful of people, or maybe even just two or three people, form a mastermind group. Meet up regularly on Zoom, motivate and inspire each other. Keep your meetings to regular times, let everyone in the group find their voice, and always be encouraging.

Hopefully, by now you are starting to think much bigger than you were before. Our thinking has to grow daily. I never have a single day go by without learning something. Listen to positive audios, read books, keep your mind on track.

If you feel down at any time, try to reverse any negative feelings by giving thanks for what you already have. Keep the positivity going, make it a habit.

You always have something to be grateful for.

Negative thinkers think negatively because it's a habit of theirs. It takes time to break a habit, so keep boosting your own positivity every single day.

I love my positive network of friends and business colleagues. We boost each other up and celebrate our successes. Be an encourager, be known as the go-to person for positivity and light. Stay away from dark corridors, these are the dark places that lurk within us. Look at life as something to enjoy, something to savor, not something to shun.

Also...

When I first started on my online marketing journey, I made the mistake of thinking that once I had created lots of 'stuff', people would actually come running to me and buy my products. This was not the case.

You have to make the moves, especially the first move. I know people don't like to do this, but get used to it. If no one made the first move, nothing would happen.

When I publish books, they don't sell themselves. Yes, Amazon helps a little, but for a new book, reviews are essential. I have to reach out to people and ask them.

I'm not 100% comfortable with doing this. Sometimes it can come across as a little bit spammy because you're in-boxing people and asking them for favors.

But I do it anyway. Sometimes people will just be glad that you have involved them. The worst thing people can do is say no. You may get the odd person who is a little bit abusive.

Once you develop the millionaire mindset, abuse just bounces off you. Remember, our aim is to be bulletproof. Nothing worries us, nothing scares us. We are invincible, we are indestructible…

The next section of this book is the practical appliance of that millionaire science. We've tackled the mindset and now it's time to tackle the practical stuff. Roll up your sleeves and let's go.

High fives all round. Congratulations for completing the mindset part. You are now a millionaire mind warrior.

Key takeaways:

- **We've covered exactly what makes a millionaire** –Are entrepreneurs born or made? It's both. If you want more money, give more value.

- **Avoiding the comfort zone** – Who named this the comfort zone?. There is nothing actually comfortable about the comfort zone, it just means staying as you are. The sooner you look outside of the box, the better.

- **The power of a mastermind group** – How masterminds are key in developing your millionaire mindset and how upgrading your friends list is a good idea. You are probably the average of your five best friends. Seek out encouragers, dump those negative nellies.

- **Make the first move** – Don't wait for people to come to you. Millionaires are people who make things happen. Reach out to others first. Swallow your pride, swallow your fears, and go in all guns blazing.

7
MARSHMALLOWS AND MONEY

"*Don't give up what you want most, for what you want now.*" – *Richard G. Scott*

You may be aware of a certain test done at Stanford University in 1972, where a study was done on children to see how delayed gratification affected a child's future behavior.

Each child was offered a marshmallow as an immediate reward but also given a choice to have two marshmallows instead if they would delay eating the first one.

Of course, kids being kids, many of them just grabbed the first marshmallow and ate it there and then. However, some children delayed eating the first marshmallow in order to get another one.

Much later.

A study was done on the children in later years. You probably don't need me to tell you that the children who exercised the willpower of delayed gratification did a lot better later on in life. Their school SAT scores, and other things like their BMI (body mass index) were taken into account, as were their successes in their careers.

I don't think there were any big surprises here. Demonstrating delayed gratification shows great willpower. People with willpower are more likely to demonstrate greater success in certain areas of their life.

Delayed gratification plays a big part in business too, although we have a picture in our minds of what the end result will look like, getting to that end result can take quite a while before it actually happens.

Many, would-be millionaires are working hard at the grind for long-term satisfaction but often they face short-term hardship as they feed their business while trying to feed their families.

This is part and parcel of becoming wealthy though. You spend money wisely on your business and often forgo a lot of the luxuries that we would normally get used to and enjoy.

You are investing in your brand new baby (your business), and you treat it with the love and care that you would if it were a real baby.

I spent years driving around in an old banger of a car that I bought from a friend for $800 before I actually made any decent money in my business. I still don't drive a top-of-the-range car, but I don't drive around in an old banger anymore either.

I got used to living within my means. This makes sense as every spare dollar you save could be making you ten dollars or more in your business.

One of the greatest feelings I have known is to be able to afford things that you don't feel the need to actually own.

This might sound crazy but just knowing that you can afford them is a very nice feeling in itself.

Keep money in the bank for emergencies. You never know when your car may need work doing on it, and always keep money aside to add additional funds to your business as and when you need it. You never know when the right opportunity will arrive.

Don't be afraid of the Magic Million.

I know a million sounds like a big figure. Think how it must have sounded to people a hundred years ago. There were millionaires way back in history who could have probably bought a whole country with their millions.

It's all relative of course. If you earn $700 a week, then a million will seem huge. If you earn $10,000 a week, then it's merely a couple of years' pay. The more we think like a millionaire, the more likely we are to achieve it.

Let's look at the reality.

Most people wouldn't think twice about selling a product online for $50. If you sell a mere twenty, you'll get paid $1000. Now, you need to scale your operation.

Instead of concentrating on the lower number ($50), look on it as a task to get forty sales at $50, which will give you $2000. Now, turn that into a game plan of completing 500 of those $2000 tasks and you will have your million.

Although a million sounds like a magic number, it's really just a very big number made up of many smaller numbers. These smaller numbers are more acceptable, as people tend to relate most of their spending to their hourly, weekly, or yearly pay.

For instance, if you spend $300 a week on household shopping, you might relate that to being a half of your weekly pay.

When we talk about a million, that amount is unfathomable to a lot of people as it could take the average person 25 years to earn it.

As I've said before, it's not about working hard. A lot of people work hard, but they don't have much to show for it after years and years of 'working hard'.

Working smart is how you get to make a million.

The reality is, if making a million was that impossible to achieve, there would only be a very small amount of people in the world actually doing it. According to Credit Suisse's Global Wealth Report of 2021, there were 56.1 million millionaires in the world at the end of 2020.

That's pretty incredible, don't you think? 56.1 million millionaires.

Planning to be rich.

This might sound pretty obvious, but you do have to plan to be rich. Although you'll often find me in front of a laptop, in my opinion, you still can't beat writing a plan with a good old-fashioned pen and pad.

The actual physical act of writing seems to stimulate a part of the brain that makes what you write down much easier to remember. I don't know if this is a medical fact but it certainly works for me. Now, at this point, you are probably thinking, "What exactly am I supposed to be writing down?"

My answer is: Your actual plan to win. Remember: Failing to plan is the same as planning to fail.

In order to reach the magic million, you need to plan each and every step, and make those steps count. This will not be a walk in the park by any means. Most books teach you what to do, but very few books teach you how to actually do it. This book covers the what and the how to.

Let's start with the plan.

The master plan.

This is the part where we get an idea of what kind of business we want to start. Write it all down.

Step 1. How much am I willing to put up with in order to get rich? Life will never be the same for you again. You can't make large sums of money and carry on your life as you live it now.

This is a common mistake. Some people want to start a business from home, but don't expect any inconvenience. There will be an ongoing inconvenience, more stress, etc. How much are you willing to put up with?

Step 2. What is my Why? Money alone should never be the No.1 reason for you wanting to start a business. Although money can buy you the things that will bring you temporary happiness, it's never going to make you permanently happy.

Think of all the benefits of having time freedom instead – this is far more valuable than the money itself.

Find your REAL why?

I sometimes ask people, "Why do you want to go into business?" Nine times out of ten, they will say, "I want to make more money."

How much is 'more money? Do you really know?

This is not your REAL why

Although people say 'more money', this is very vague. Imagine trying to hit a 'vague' target.

Ask yourself better questions.

"How much exactly is more money?" Start to think and act in a more focused way.

OK, so you give me this crazy figure: $2,856,000 and fifty cents. After I laugh at your precise figure, I ask;

"If you make all this money, then what?"

You reply, "Well, if I made $2,856,000 and fifty cents, I could give up work."

I then ask you, "And if you gave up work, then what would you do?" The point of this exercise is to keep drilling down until you reach your real why. You can't hit a target if you don't know what it is.

Step 3. What am I good at? Think about your hobbies, your job, etc. What skills do you have? Maybe you write well, maybe you are a born salesman, perhaps you are good at bookkeeping. Write it all down on paper. This is called a brain dump. You are downloading your ideas from brain to paper.

Step 4. What do I love doing? What you are good at and what you love doing, might not be the same thing.

e.g. I love hiking, I love to write, I love helping people.

A lot of people tell you to follow your passion. I know this is common in a lot of self-help books, but you don't have to follow your passion to make a million. Your passion might be something that won't make you a penny. Get passionate about making money.

Once you make enough money, you can follow your passion all day long. Until then, be passionate about making your first million.

Key takeaways:

- **We spoke about delayed gratification** – We talked about how important this is in building your business. We also highlighted the 1972 Stanford University experiment on children who were asked to delay their gratification by choosing two marshmallows at a later time or having one now. The results of this study were amazing.

- **We talked about how important it is to have a plan** – Failing to plan is like planning to fail. Write it all down, keep pen and paper with you at all times, you never know when a great idea will arrive.

- **We talked about what your REAL why is** – It's often not what you think it is at first thought. Most people don't know what their real WHY is until they keep drilling down. It's in there somewhere, it's up to you to keep asking yourself questions until you find it.

- **We also talked about what are you really good at** – This is so important when starting a business. You don't have to 'follow your passion', not in business anyway.

But it helps that whatever you choose to do in business is something that you actually like doing. Otherwise, you may get bored after a while and just quit.

8
SHOW ME THE MONEY

If you don't find a way to make money while you sleep, you'll work until you die." – Warren Buffett

Now that your brain has been sufficiently fried, we come to the part of the book that turns all of that good thinking into action. "Hurrah!" you say.

But first. Let's talk about ego.

Do you want to be right, or do you want to be rich?

I think we all have a bit of an ego. This egotistical view of things can sometimes be our worst enemy. I know that during the last 40 years of being a serial entrepreneur, I have been wrong a lot more times than I've been right.

Why?

Well, for a start, if you are out there in the trenches making lots of decisions, the law of averages tells you that some of those decisions are going to be wrong. Your job is to put those wrong decisions behind you and keep making decisions anyway.

Don't expect to be right every time. Sometimes, our ego gets in the way and we end up making bad decisions because of our need to be right.

Probably my No.1 fault was thinking that I knew it all.

Sometimes, when you create a little success here and there, it leads to arrogance. You start to believe your own #BS. I thought I knew more than I actually did and I wouldn't listen to other people.

This is quite common. Although we are entrepreneurs, we should always remain open to advice. We are no better than anyone else, we just know a little bit more than some.

The truth is, we can all learn something from other people. This is how you learn anything in life. It's true we learn from our own mistakes, but mistakes can be expensive, it's cheaper to learn from the mistakes of others.

If you are 30, 40, 50, 60+, etc., you can still learn a lot from people who are much younger. Don't write anyone off just because of their age, there is a lot of valuable knowledge out there to be learned from people younger and older than you.

Although we associate wisdom with age, often or not, younger people can be extremely wise for their age.

Bad examples.

Even bad examples can teach us how not to do something. It's important to keep an open mind.

I don't think any of us wants to be wrong, but wanting to be right all the time often leads to failure. Most arrogant people end up with a big ego, but a very small bank account.

We have two ears and one mouth for a reason. We learn more by listening than talking. Some people just want to out-talk you and they never listen. They just wait for you to take a breath so that they can speak.

Always be a good listener.

Million Dollar Factoid.

There are a million ways to make a million dollars. The world is full of ideas. No matter what shortages you have in your life, ideas should not be one of them.

You can make a million dollars selling toilet paper. It doesn't have to be a prestigious type of business to make prestigious money. But, always start a business that resonates with you.

Start a business that you can actually see yourself doing, day in and day out, for the foreseeable future. Start a business that you can be enthusiastic about even when things go wrong. Remember, a business is a long-term commitment.

So many people start a business and give up in just a few weeks or months because it doesn't go to plan. This is crazy. Your business can change your whole life and the lives of your family forever. Why would you give up something so valuable, so soon?.

Here in the UK, 60% of all start-up businesses are gone by the end of their third year. Why?

The five most common causes of business failure:

1. No business plan.

You can't run a business solely on enthusiasm. It's a nice concept but it's not a reality. You need to create a solid business plan. Create a plan from your goals and your calculated projections, at least for the first year.

Think of your business plan as a roadmap. Every business needs structure. Your business plan will keep you accountable, plus it will keep you on track if you start to veer off the path.

Remember what I said earlier. Not having a plan is actually planning to fail.

2. Not enough capital.

People often oversimplify the process of making money. They frequently have unrealistic expectations of when they will be profitable. I have news for you. I don't expect my publishing business to make a profit in its first year. In fact, it will probably lose money.

Would I give it up? I think you know the answer to that. NEVER!

Give your business time to breathe. It's your baby, and we love babies. Treat your business just like your newborn. Care for it, look after it, watch it, and help it grow.

3. Running out of cash.

If you are running your business part-time while you are holding down a job, this shouldn't worry you too much as you can always earn more money. However, make sure that you have good access to capital, allow for your business to be unprofitable for a while.

For the first few months, or even the first year or two, you will probably be paying out a lot more than you take in.

4. Not understanding the market.

You need to know who your ideal customer is. You need to know their buying habits and you also need to know when and how they buy. You would be surprised at just how little research gets done on this by the average business owner. Find out who is likely to be the person to buy your product.

We need to know who they are and we need to be able profile that person so we can target them in our advertising, and in our product presentation.

5. Not having a backup plan.

If it all goes wrong, then what? Some people will give up at the very first sign of trouble. Don't let this be you. Have a plan 'B'. You need a backup plan just in case plan 'A' isn't working out.

This could be in the form of a different way to present the same business, or it could be in the form of a spare amount of cash to introduce to your business. Whatever it is, always have that plan B.

Money loves speed.

This means money likes action NOW! It doesn't like being kept waiting while you try to make it perfect. Perfection is slow and unattainable, but many people still dabble in it. Get your money working now.

As an example. If you are publishing books, some of the best authors in the world are non-perfectionists. Whilst they are out there writing and selling book after book, the perfectionist hasn't even finished the first book.

This applies to anything you do. Start now, and let it go when it's good enough.

Here is how I speed up my day, and you should adopt this too if you intend to make a million.

Remember when you arrive at your job, you chinwag with your colleagues and maybe have a coffee, you then scratch your butt and hang out a bit more, then you decide to start work. Well, making a million and working for yourself is not like that.

You are the boss now. You are the one making all the decisions and you have to motivate yourself. Time is money and if you are wasting time, it's probably costing you money. This is what I do each day.

Steps to speed up your day.

Step 1. Before you go to bed each night, create a list of all the things that need to be done the very next day. Give a certain amount of time for each task and write those tasks into your diary or planner. Put the most important, or the task you are the most resistant to, first in the list. Fresh eyes and a fresh mind will make that task a lot easier.

Step 2. Get up early. Yes, I know it's Sunday and you used to lie in till 12.00, but now it's different. Money never sleeps. Get enough good sleep so that you don't become a zombie, but don't overdo it.

Exercise and meditation.

Exercising each morning, even if it's only for twenty minutes will help wake you up. A fifteen-minute session of meditation after your exercise will help calm your mind and set you up for the day.

I also like to write in my journal each day, I write all my personal stuff down, and I keep a record of what's going on in my life at present for future reference. Drink plenty of water to stay hydrated. A lot of the time, tiredness comes down to a lack of hydration.

Practice deep breathing exercises (The Wim Hoff method springs to mind). This will also help reduce tiredness by making sure your body is properly oxygenated.

You are now prepping yourself to have a good start to the day.

Step 3. Sit down and complete each task you have written down on your list in the allotted time without any distractions. Turn off any distractions such as the TV and any smartphone notifications.

Don't get up off of your chair until you have completed each task. Think back to our previous lesson on focus? This is you now putting that lesson into practice.

I do this morning ritual every day. When I'm writing a book, I allow two hours per day to write. I do this undisturbed, regardless of what else is going on in my world. Obviously, bathroom breaks and coffee breaks are needed but don't get distracted into doing anything else while you are in the flow of things.

Go forth and multiply.

Our next step in the money loves speed phase is to get into an almost 'production line' mentality.

Hopefully, by now, you are out of the procrastination phase and you are in the taking massive action phase. It takes a lot of action on your part to get massive results.

The idea is to spread a web of products and services across the Internet. There are billions of potential customers.

Let's move on to the next chapter where we will be looking at which business to start. We are well on the road to freedom now. All of the chapters up until now have been your guiding Sat-Nav, now we are going to concentrate on the vehicle.

Key takeaways:

• **We talked about whether you want to be right or rich** – Our ego can easily stop us from progressing if we can't see past ourselves. We must be prepared to listen to others.

Even if you have years of experience, there is always something you can learn from others.

Don't discount something just because the person who told you it is young. Some of the best ideas come from young people.

• **We looked at the five most common causes of business failure** – This ranged from having no business plan to not even having a backup plan. Don't be one of those people.

• **We also talked about how money loves speed** – Learning how to be more productive ourselves is the key to producing more goods and services and, ultimately, more sales and profit.

9
THE MILLION DOLLAR BUSINESS

lways deliver more than expected."– Larry Page, Founder of Google

A OK, I know it sounds like a good idea, Spending time with your laptop open on the beach, thinking of all the ways that you can spend all that money. It sounds like a dream come true lifestyle, but anyone who has actually attempted to do this will tell you that it is seriously flawed.

Despite people's attempts on social media to make the laptop lifestyle look like a non-stop adventure of fun, drinking Tequila on the beach whilst millions of dollars keep pouring into your laptop, I've got news for you.

Usually, you can't even see anything on the screen of a laptop on the beach because the glare from the sun is so strong. Many beaches have no, or very poor internet connections and sand can do an awful lot of damage to your computer. Sorry to disappoint you, but it is what it is.

Laptops and beaches don't usually mix very well.

However, the laptop lifestyle really can be an amazing experience if this is one of your goals. I have friends who do this and according to them it's a great life. You really can make money while traveling the world at the same time.

Whatever your main reason is to make your million, embrace the journey and go for it. You don't need to stop at making one million; you can achieve much, much more than that. If you can make one million dollars, you can make 10 or 20, etc. There are no limits.

In today's world, a million dollars, pounds, or euros won't be enough to retire on unless perhaps you are over sixty. People are living much longer these days, so we need a lot more money than before.

Money should be used to create more money. If we spend everything we make, we will have to keep working forever.

This is why working for someone else is often described as being on a hamster wheel. I know this sounds a little unkind, but many people in a job do feel like they are spinning their wheels, they do feel like they are getting nowhere.

According to the World Economic Forum, in 2021, 40% of employed workers are thinking of changing their jobs. This is despite the uncertainty that has been caused by the pandemic.

A job is a bit like living 40 to 50 years of your life on repeat. This kind of life doesn't leave a lot of time for actually living, and although it's a convenient life for many, I wouldn't say it was living your best life.

I don't think we were just put on this earth just to pay bills, retire, and then expire, do you?

Assuming that we only get one life, are you still prepared to give up most of it to an employer? I personally wasn't. Don't get me wrong, a job serves a purpose, but as you know, life flashes past very quickly and it is our choice how we spend it.

Let's choose a business.

Step 1. Hopefully, you have thought over the type of business that is right for you. You probably have an idea of what you can see yourself doing for the next few months and years. Maybe it's selling a product or perhaps it's creating a service.

Step 2. As discussed earlier, we now have a plan in front of us and a budget to use for our capital. Don't skimp on this; it's better to have too much money in the kitty than not enough. You don't want to run out of money halfway through the year.

Step 3. Hopefully, your expectations are realistic and you are not expecting a golden eagle to shower dollars from the sky onto your head. This is your dream that you are now putting into action, so be prepared to work hard at it.

Step 4. If you are planning to do this while holding down a job, plan your spare time accordingly. Make sure that you are allowing a decent amount of time each day to work on your business.

Just because you work in your job for five days a week, remember that working for yourself is different. It's often a seven-day-a-week thing, at least for the early stages of your business, so no slacking.

If you are going to do this full time, create your six or seven-day-a-week plan meticulously and allow yourself some breathing space each day for working on your health and wellbeing.

A lot of millionaires meditate in the morning and hit the gym at least two or three times a week. If the gym doesn't turn you on, then a daily brisk walk early in the morning will help get those creative juices flowing.

For more ideas for your daily early morning routine, look up any 'Miracle Morning' book on Amazon from Hal Elrod. He knows a thing or two about morning routines.

It looks like we are now fully functioning in the brain department and we are all powered up and ready to go. It's now time to blast off and make that million.

Let's go.

I am going to give you two very good online business ideas that you may want to investigate. These are two, very solid current ideas I really suggest you take a good look at.

I've picked these two as they are very much ripe for today's consumer market, plus you can scale them to the moon and back.

Both of these business ideas have the capability to create that magic million on their own, or they could simply add another profitable string of income to your existing business if you have one.

Business 1. The Self-Publishing Business.

I am very proud of this business; this is the business I personally do. You may have guessed that already as you are reading one of my books.

A book written and published by you is probably the best business card you could ever give to someone. It portrays you as a professional, it opens a lot of doors, and your prospective customer is far more likely to buy from you if contact comes via a book that you have published.

Many successful people are publishing books as a lead to their other products. You may have seen the ads on Facebook where you are offered a book for the shipping costs only.

Once you receive that book, you are then offered their back-end coaching services which they mention in the book itself.

Many people shy away from writing a book because they think it's beyond them. This couldn't be further from the truth. I know there is an old saying that has been going around for years that *'everyone has at least one good book in them'*.

This is true.

In reality, everyone probably has more than one good book in them. There are plenty of good books out there that can teach you how to write a book. If you can write, with practice, you can write a book.

I wrote a book called 'How To Write a Book' solely for this purpose. To teach people from scratch to write one.

Before I wrote my first book, the only real writing I had ever done since my early school days was to blog. It was a big jump going from blogging to actually writing a book, but after a lot of procrastinating and worrying about whether it would be good enough, I completed my first book and I launched it.

That book was called 'Money Mind Crush' and I'm very glad I did it. The book sells very well on Amazon.

You can do exactly the same.

I know people who have gone from having a job to creating a self-publishing business empire with dozens of books, turning over thousands of dollars a month. There is absolutely no limit to what you can earn with self-publishing.

The good thing is that with a platform like Amazon, the traffic is already there, and it's all buyer traffic. People go on to Amazon to buy things, not just to browse. In order to be seen on Amazon, you will also need to do some marketing yourself. However, Amazon also has its own ad platform which can work very well if you know what you are doing.

Once you have created your book. You need a good catchy title and subtitle. Amazon's search is like any search engine: people type in the keyword to the books they want to browse. If you give your book an obscure title, the chances are no one will find it. Make sure your title has your main keyword in where possible and add keywords to your subtitle.

Create a good-looking cover for your book and now you're almost ready to publish on KDP Kindle Direct Publishing (Amazon).

You publish your book as a Kindle Book and enrol it in the Kindle Unlimited program. This KU program is where people borrow your book and you get paid for every page that they read. This all adds up. You are not only getting paid on book sales, but also for page reads too.

Next, you publish your book as a paperback. The sale price of this will be higher as you have printing costs to factor in. Amazon publishes your paperback on a print-on-demand basis.

You don't have to keep any stock of the book. Amazon prints your book when the customer buys it and sends it direct to your customer.

Now what?

Remember me talking about 'Money Loves Speed? Well, you simply keep things moving. Take the manuscript of your book and upload it to ACX. This is the publishing platform for Audible. Yes, you are now going to turn your book into an Audiobook.

You will need to hire a narrator for this job unless you possess these skills yourself and you have some good equipment to record on. The going rate for hiring a narrator varies but you can expect to pay between $50 -$100 per hour of recording time.

A 30,000-word book will take about three hours of recording time, so you'll need to budget around $150 -$300 to turn that book of yours into an audiobook.

Plus, you will need to create an audiobook cover.

I always get the person who created my paperback and eBook cover to do an audiobook cover too.

Once you have completed this process, there is nothing stopping you from creating a hardback version of your book for even more profit.

I've given you a brief overview of the self-publishing business. It can be very profitable and also a very satisfying business to be in. You can add a self-publishing business to almost any business that you are currently in, linking each book you publish to your email list and sales funnel.

Use your books to promote affiliate products.

You can also use your books to promote other products too, like a high ticket coaching program. Sometimes, your books can make more money by doing this than by the actual book sales themselves.

This is the model I use personally. Every step I've explained here is what I am actually doing myself. I don't have a high ticket coaching program yet but it's on the cards. I do sell other products from within my books though. Books are a great way of selling affiliate products too, you simply include a link within the book.

Obviously, this is easier to do with Kindle eBooks than it is with a paperback, as you can add a clickable link in an eBook.

However, you can still point people toward a link in a paperback, it just requires a little more effort on the reader's part.

The self-publishing business has massive potential.

People have an insatiable appetite for information. If you can present that information to people with your own unique slant on it and give people answers to the problems they have, you can really clean up by doing self-publishing.

This business has two very big plus points:

1. It's very scalable. You can start by publishing one book. You can learn from your mistakes as you go, publish another book, then another. Publishing businesses are not only very scalable but they are also very saleable too.

If you go over to empireflippers.com, you will see many digital businesses being advertised for sale for 30, 40, and even 50 times their monthly net profit. People love to buy a ready-made publishing business as it doesn't take a lot of maintenance once it's up and running.

This would mean that if you decided to sell your publishing business after, say, two or three years, if you were making $20,000 per month in profit (many are doing this), with a 40 x multiple, you would have a business worth $800,000, and with a 50 x multiple. BOOM!, you've reached the magic million.

This is all very possible.

2. It's a high-demand, low-cost entry-level, all-year-round business that you can operate it easily from home. All you need to get started is a book idea, some time to write, a little bit of cash to get a decent book cover made (or make one yourself), and that's about it

Business 2. The Print On Demand Business.

Although self-publishing is also a print-on-demand business, the actual print-on-demand business we are talking about here is not books. It's mugs, T-shirts, and basically anything you can print a design onto. I would suggest starting with one type of item to kick off your print-on-demand business. Let's start with mugs.

Who doesn't love a mug?. Mugs are pretty much used by nearly everyone on the planet. And the good thing about a mug is, people tend to have lots of them. For instance, a family of five people might have ten or even as many as twenty mugs in the house.

People also love mugs that have designs on them.

When running a print-on-demand business, we don't actually do any of the printing ourselves. Our job is to create the designs and find the customers. That's it. Our first step here is to find a company that will handle all of our print-on-demand needs.

The Printer.

There are many online companies that will carry out this work for you. They print your design, then they send the newly designed mug to your customer in protective wrapping for a safe, smash-free delivery.

When selecting a print-on-demand company, do your due diligence. You will want quality and you want reliability. Choose a company that has lots of good feedback. Check out their website and also check on Google to see what people are saying about that company.

You want a long-term business relationship with the printer that includes good communication, good quality printing, and, of course, a good delivery service for your products.

Two very well known companies who print designs on mugs and deliver them are:

Printify: https://printify.com

Gelato: https://gelato.com

There are many more, and I suggest you investigate both of these companies further before deciding to deal with them.

Print On Demand – The Design.

Let's talk about the design process next. Personally, I'm not a designer or a graphic artist and I don't think many people who operate a print-on-demand business are. Most people either get their designs done for them on sites like Fiverr.com or they use software such as brushyourideas.com to make their designs.

There are many different apps and online design products capable of creating professional designs. Just type into Google, 'Best Mug Design Software' to get a list of companies supplying these.

Once you have created your very first design and you have your print-on-demand printer in place, you will now want to know how to sell your mugs.

Print On Demand – The Selling Process.

As I said earlier, there is pretty much an unquenchable thirst for mugs with designs on them. Think about a day trip you may have taken to the Tower of London, or to your favorite theme park. The chances are, there would be opportunities to buy mugs, T-shirts, phone cases, etc, with the logo or design of that venue printed on it.

A word of warning here. Create your own designs, don't copy other people's designs. You may end up in court facing serious charges.

People love to have things that remind them of good times. People love to have 'stuff' with funny, crazy, or funky designs on them.

You can sell print-on-demand products from your own eCom platform or choose a platform that already has traffic going to it. Etsy (https://www.etsy.com/) is a good place to start.

Etsy is an arty type marketplace, unlike eBay. eBay sells all kinds of products, cars, gym equipment, etc., but Etsy is a different kettle of fish. It's designed to sell more craft-like types of products. The gift market, in general, is huge and people don't need much of an excuse to buy gifts.

There are lots of people who just like having funky mugs around the home. I know I do. Your products will get a huge boost of sales in the holiday season if you make them holiday-related, for example, Halloween, Christmas. etc.

From here, you can simply increase your designs and increase your gift ideas. You may also want to add T-shirts to your product line. Always remember though that T-shirts have different sizes, so you may get more refunds and returns from people who have ordered the wrong size.

The good thing is, the print-on-demand company deals with all the printing and delivery. This takes a lot of weight off of the shoulders of the business owner.

I highly recommend Print-On-Demand as a low-cost business to start. The initial outlay is modest and the potential for making good profits is very high. Many people are making six figures a year and more from this type of business model.

Can you scale it up? Absolutely, there is absolutely nothing stopping you from scaling this business to $20,000 a month and more, and selling it on Empire Flippers for a cool million dollars.

Once you know how to create products and sell them, you can increase your revenue a lot further by simply telling others how to do the same.

You will of course charge for this service.

1. Create books on either or both of the two businesses mentioned above, explaining how you have created a profitable business. Never be afraid of creating more competition; there are billions of customers in the world. You won't affect your current business by telling others how to do it for themselves. But you will be increasing your profits. Always think with an abundance mindset.

2. Create a video course on how to do either, or both businesses. Sell it as a high-ticket item. People are willing to spend upwards of $1000 for a good program showing them how to do this.

P.S. I recently spent $1000 on a course teaching me how to create a publishing business. This was money well spent.

People are hungry for good information. After all, isn't that why you are reading this book?

People long to quit their job and work from home for themselves. The two businesses I've described above are, by far (in my opinion) two of the best businesses out there for creating a full-time income. Both can be run from home and both have the capability of getting you much closer to that million.

In the next chapter, I will be discussing the secret of 'compounding'. This is how to accelerate your capital to make even more. People have used this method to make fortunes for centuries.

Key takeaways:

- **We discussed why $1,000,000** probably won't get you very far these days and that $10,000,000 is probably a much better figure to aim for if you intend to be financially free for the rest of your life

- **We talked about two very good business ideas that ACTUALLY work** – In my opinion, these are two of the best opportunities around today. If you are not too keen on writing a book then you most definitely want to do the other one, Print-on-Demand. I wouldn't suggest doing both at once as that's like chasing two rabbits. Concentrate on one business at a time and do that well.

See you in the next chapter. This one is a biggie. It's all about compounding your profits.

10
COMPOUND OR DIE

"*Compound interest is the eighth wonder of the world. He who understands it, earns it; he who doesn't, pays it.*" – *Albert Einstein*

You may have heard the above quote before.

Compounding is often spoken about when it comes to the interest paid on a person's savings account. Maybe you are getting a lousy 0.01% interest per year on your savings, should you leave the interest in the account to compound or should you put it somewhere else where it will grow faster?

I'm not qualified to give financial advice but if it were me, I would be asking myself, "surely if I invested that money in my own business, couldn't I beat that lousy interest rate?".

How do we use compounding in business?

If you are starting, or you are already running a business and you put that money into your business, and then you keep re-investing it back in, you are naturally compounding that money.

By consistently reinvesting those profits, we are allowing those profits to compound, and by using that extra capital to buy business assets or increased advertising, this should create more profit.

Let me give you an example.

My dear old dad remarried and set up a home in the town of Epping, in Essex, England. He moved in with my step-mum and between them, they formed a company selling electrical components. These components were used in fruit machines (one-armed bandits).

After a few months, the business started to prosper. At this stage, my dad was 65 years of age and was also getting his pension. He kept reinvesting the profit they made from the business back into new stock and the business continued to grow.

Eventually, his neighbors got so fed up with delivery lorries pulling up at all hours outside their houses and blocking their driveways, they complained to the council. My dad and step-mum moved their business into commercial premises in nearby Harlow, Essex.

Next door to their industrial unit was a sign-making business operated by two young guys. My dad got on really well with them.

The business that these two guys had was very profitable, but they spent most of the profits on two company Mercedes cars and various other items not conducive to making their company any money.

Within a couple of years, their sign-making business had gone bust. Spending outweighed their income and this was a sure sign (forgive the pun) of impending doom for their business.

My dad was sad to see these two guys go out of business. He did try to give them some friendly advice, but the 'pull' of the money got the better of them and they spent everything that the company made (and more).

Result: They went bankrupt.

Investing money back into your business is the key to longevity.

Let the profits compound and make more profit. There is always a temptation to take money out early and buy nice things. However, every dollar you take out of your business now could be taking hundreds, if not thousands of dollars out of it in the future if the money is not allowed to create more profits and compound.

People have started businesses with very small amounts of capital and they've just reinvested each and every dollar back into the business. This is how you can truly scale up and build a million-dollar business.

You have to make money work for you.

Key takeaways:

- **We talked about my dad's business** – He didn't start it until he was 65 and retired. He never took any money out of the business during its first year or so, he lived off his pension, my stepmom and my dad moved the business out of their home once it started to grow.

- **We also talked about the importance of investing the profit** back into the business. An example of not doing that was shown by the two guys who owned the business next door to my dad's industrial unit. They went bust after only a couple of years of being in business, by basically spending all of the company's profits on flash cars and other things that didn't benefit the business.

11
I HAVE NO MONEY, BUT I'M OPEN TO OFFERS

"*Wealth is not about having a lot of money. It's about having a lot of options.*" – *Chris Rock*

This chapter ties in very nicely with the last one. The reason is, you can start small with a very modest amount of money and compound that capital to grow into a very large, profitable business.

Here's how.

Firstly, there is no shame in not having any money. I've been there many, many times.

Being skint, broke, pot-less, brassic, whatever you wish to call the art of having no money, it is no fun when it happens to you, but it happens to the best of us at some time or other.

Your self-worth and your net worth are not connected. You may feel better by having a lot of money in the bank, but if you don't have it, it doesn't make you worth any less. It's all in our minds when we equate what we have with what we are.

If I was to sell you as a person, I could probably get more than a million dollars in spare parts alone.

Jokes aside...

In this chapter, I want to address a fallacy that many people have about business. One of the reasons why many people don't ever start a business is that they don't think they have enough money to do so.

I can understand why people think like this, but in truth, this is not the actual reason. If you truly don't have the money to start a business, what you are actually lacking is a strategy.

What strategy? I hear you ask

The strategy to turn your time or something you own into start-up capital. If you don't have the capital, you need to be more resourceful.

Here's how I went from zero capital to $50,000 a year with no actual start-up capital. And trust me when I say this, if I can do this, so can you.

It was Christmas 2003.

I had just had my 'final' holiday in Fort Lauderdale, Florida. It was a very hot and sweaty 80 degrees in Florida, it was November, and I was about to board the plane for Heathrow, London.

I say 'final holiday' because I was contemplating getting out of a JOB and focusing again on creating a brand new business. The tolerance I have for working for a boss is very low.

I hated most of my jobs.

In my own mind, I had already decided to quit my job and just concentrate on being self-employed again. A job, to me, was a kind of a convenient inconvenience. I was never really a good fit for the pay as your earn life, I hated being told what to do and told when I could take time off for holidays. I use jobs as a means to live and pay bills while I try to figure out what my next business will be.

My holiday in Florida was expensive, and wiped out most of my savings, but I came back to England full of enthusiasm for starting my brand new venture. By the way, I hadn't decided what that new venture was to be yet.

I had enough money to pay the mortgage for the month of December. I could see January of the coming year being a tight one for cash. And then I did something completely crazy. I just went ahead and quit my job.

I'm not recommending anyone else should do something this crazy on the spur of the moment, especially without any back- up funds.

So, there I was. Christmas 2003, and no job. I had a fairly large mortgage and absolutely no income to speak of. Was I totally mad?

You might call me crazy, but for me, my thinking had changed. When you have a weekly or monthly salary arriving like clockwork you don't have to make that move, and a lot of people don't.

Most people only move when the alarm bells start ringing, like when they get fired or made redundant.

When you burn your bridges behind you, your thinking switches from "maybe I will" to "now I have to." When that switch clicks over in your head, your subconscious now goes into overdrive to find a solution.

Your best ideas will come to you when you are not actively thinking at all. Let your subconscious think for you.

You are like a heat-seeking missile, you will do anything and everything to get money back into your bank account if you see it pouring out like a leaky bucket. Sometimes the best thing that can happen to you is to hit rock bottom first. Then, the only way you can go is up.

And then, in that moment, I knew I could do this.

After what seemed to be a very long and boring Christmas, I was ready to get resourceful and start turning things around. No matter how many times you get stuck, there is always a solution.

I looked around the house for things to sell. I had accumulated a very large book collection over the years. This was all of my personal development and business books. I had been collecting these since I was about 13.

I thought to myself, "It's nice having all these books around the house but it won't pay the bills. It's time to sell." So, I sold them, all of them to one person on eBay. I got $350 (£250).

This money was going to be the seed capital for my next venture. But, what venture, you may ask?

"I know. Why not sell stuff on eBay?" After all, I had just sold my books on there for $350.

BOOM! Off we go.

It was January 2004. What do people normally buy in January?.

It didn't take that long to decide. I scouted through what seemed like hundreds and hundreds of pages of product ads on eBay. I spend hours, literally hours looking at listings, looking at products, looking at the feedback. Then I decided.

"I'm going to sell diet pills."

And so the journey began. I located a supplier of diet pills in the USA via Google. I ordered two boxes of the damn things. I went on to the company's website and got their permission to use some of their product images for my eBay ads.

Two very large boxes turned up a week later via UPS. And there I was, off to the races.

Was it a success?

You decide.

I was making sales hand over fist in January. People were buying one, two, or three bottles at a time. I created special offers, buy 2 get 1 free etc. I thought possibly that I might see a slowdown in February as many people often quit their New Year's resolutions around that time.

But. No, It just kept on going and going

Diet pills were HOT!!!

By April, I was awarded "Gold Powerseller" status by eBay. Back then, this meant that you were shifting about £6,000 (about $8250) worth of products per month, or you sold so many thousand units – I can't remember the exact numbers. 2004 was a long time ago.

Business was booming.

This is what I mean by being resourceful. You might not have the actual money in cash right now in your pocket, but you probably have something that you can sell to use as your seed capital.

That business lasted three years and made me more than $150,000. All of this from a small $350 investment. Those personal development books that were gathering dust on my shelves saved the day. What could you sell right now to finance your next business?

Have a think.

The money is there. We all own something, right? When you sell it, don't pocket that money and spend it, use it to make more money.

Develop this habit from now on, It's an important element toward your success.

Here's another idea to make you money with very little start-up capital.

Become a Gig Broker

This is something I've done in the past to make some pretty easy money. I go into it in a bit more detail over here on my blog: https://keitheverett.co.uk or visit the resources in the back of this book for the actual link.

This is how you do it:

Step 1. Open an account with Fiverr and Upwork.

Step 2. Find a service that you can offer from a seller on Fiverr and offer the same service at a higher price on Upwork.

Step 3. Use the money that you collect from the buyer on Upwork and pay your seller on Fiverr when they complete the job. You then keep the difference.

Brokers can make a lot of money. So can you with this very clever plan.

As an example, your very first product could be a book cover. These are always in high demand. There is no end of new books being created every day. They all need a cover.

No design skills? Don't worry.

You're not actually going to do any of the design work yourself. You are simply an intermediary between the two parties. You are the broker.

When you advertise your book cover design gig on Upwork, people will probably want to see samples. You show the same samples that your seller on Fiverr displays on his ad. When the buyer on Upwork orders the gig, you send the details to your seller on Fiverr to fulfill.

He/she designs the book cover for, let's say somewhere between $10 & $25. The price you set on Upwork is anywhere between $50 & $75

I always look for the best sellers to deal with on Fiverr. Don't skimp on this. Look for reliable Level 1 or 2 sellers only. Also, I always tell them what I'm doing. I tell them I am the intermediary. This lets the Fiverr seller know that I need their finished design first, delivered to me via email, without the Fiverr logo watermark on it.

You don't want your buyer on Upwork knowing that you are getting the designs done on Fiverr. This is a perfectly legal and honest business, you are simply providing a service and both parties that you deal with are gaining from it. As are you.

Fiverr puts a watermark across the finished designs until you are happy and until you pay the seller. This doesn't help us much as a broker, so speak to the seller on Fiverr first, give him a small deposit (the price of one of his gigs). This way he will trust you not to run off with the design and not pay him.

The great thing about being a gig broker is that you can do this with many services. You don't have to just offer a book cover service. You can sell websites, image fixing services, web traffic & SEO services. The potential for high profit doing this, is huge.

You can set yourself up to do this for very little outlay. If you sell your book cover designs on Upwork for $75, Upwork charges you 20% for selling them so you'll net $60. If your Fiverr seller charges you $25, you've still made $35 for doing very little work.

What did you have to do to earn that $35? You sent a couple of emails and you answered a couple of messages. Money is everywhere. Be resourceful. The world is a very abundant place.

Key takeaways:

- **I talked about the fact that there is no shame at all in not having money** – Most entrepreneurs have been broke at some stage. I've seen many millionaires go broke, it happens. I've also been there. It's not nice.

- **I was talking about my adventures on eBay** – This platform can be a great place to make money. We all have stuff lying around the house or garage that we can sell and turn into seed capital. In this case, I turned $350 (£250) worth of books into $150,000 over three years.

- **The power of being a Gig Broker** – This is a fairly simple, straightforward business that has worked well for me in the past and can work for you too. The good thing about this business is that it requires no skill at all, and very little capital to start.

See you in the next chapter. I hope by now that the ideas are starting to flood into your mind. We can start simple businesses and scale them into huge empires over time if we keep adding income streams, and keep compounding those profits.

This leads us nicely into our next chapter: Multiple Streams of Income.

. . .

12

MULTIPLE STREAMS OF INCOME

"*There is no security in a job, even a high-paying one. Be smart and don't rely on just one source of income.*" – *Ray Higdon*

Don't you just love the sound of those words 'multiple streams of income'? I know I do. There is a kind of magical ring to it. Now, you might be thinking, "A few chapters back, he was telling me to focus, now he's talking about multiple streams of income. Which is it?"

Both, of course.

Focus on one business, but build several streams of income from it.

We often hear that millionaires have an average of seven streams of income, and I'm not disputing that. But, did they have them all in the beginning? I doubt it.

Diversifying is the devil if you make a habit of it in the beginning. Please listen to this, as it's very important. One of the biggest mistakes I've seen people do online is to diversify at the bottom, hoping that at least one of those income streams will work and make them some money.

This is what I call the scattergun effect. It's not really a plan, it's a bit like throwing darts at a dartboard in a dark alley, hoping one will hit the bullseye.

When entrepreneurs have multiple streams of income, they usually diversify at the top, not the bottom. This means that they get very good at one thing first before starting another income stream. You can't be good at everything. Get very good at one thing.

Richard Branson is a good example of this. I don't know how many companies Virgin owns at the moment, but at the last count, it was around forty.

It wasn't like that in the beginning. The first Virgin company was Virgin Music. Richard Branson ran this for years before other companies followed. Imagine if he had tried to run several companies at once in the beginning: he probably wouldn't have been as successful as he is today.

He creates companies and gets other people to run them. He's not juggling everything himself.

Sometimes, less is more.

I know people in my industry (self-publishing), who started out writing books in multiple niches. It was a logistical nightmare. This just leads to confusion. People end up going around and around in circles when they try to do too many different things at once.

Stick to one niche and grow your business from there. Don't start businesses in multiple niches – you'll be forever playing catch-up.

You might be reading this book as a paperback or a Kindle book, but did you know that it's probably available as a hardback and as an audiobook too? That's four separate streams of income without any lack of focus or too much extra work.

This is how you want to think when it comes to expanding your business and having multiple streams of income. Create the first product or service, expand that and then add related products and services.

Let me give you another example.

The Print on Demand Business

You start off by putting your designs on mugs. You get good at this and you create a large customer list. You then pick another modality to add your designs to. This could be T-shirts, or smartphone cases. You now have two or three different streams of income.

A year or two later, once you have a lot of experience under your belt (belts are good for designs too), you can now put your knowledge down on paper and teach others how to create a business like yours.

- You could create a whole series of books on the print-on-demand business and put them on Amazon for sale. You could then turn your books into audiobooks and put them on Audible.

- You could even create a digital course and sell it for a premium price.

- You could do group coaching via a weekly Zoom call.

- You could even do one-on-one coaching.

I think you get my point. You don't have to step outside of what you are already doing to create more streams of income. Create from within.

Can you see where I'm going with this? There are no limits to what you can achieve.

Affiliate Marketing.

This is a very simple business model and it helps more people get started online than probably any other business model. You can get started in affiliate marketing on a very low budget.

Affiliate marketing is simply selling someone else's product or service and then receiving a commission on the sale. You don't have to deliver the product, you don't have to worry about customer service, you simply sell and then collect the commission.

People love this business because it's very easy to get started.

To become an affiliate of digital products, simply type into Google the following three websites one at a time: Clickbank, JVZoo, and Warriorplus. Each of these websites has been in business a long time and offers good digital products that you can sell on commission.

Or go over to Muncheye.com to find out about upcoming product launches, and contact the vendors directly.

In 2010, I used this type of business to create an income stream for my blog. I was quite new to digital marketing back then, I used to give out money-making tips on my blog and link each post to a paid product related to whatever I was talking about in the post.

For instance, if I was talking about which was the best way to do email marketing, I would explain to the reader that they needed an autoresponder. An autoresponder is a piece of software they can use to send emails to their prospects in a logical sequence, automatically when someone joins their email list.

Everyone who is involved in online marketing needs to build an email list, so everyone in online marketing is a potential customer. I would join the affiliate programs from various companies such as Get Response or Aweber, and then I would do a comparison post on who was the best.

The reader would often click on the links and, on occasion, they would sign up for one of the programs. I would then receive a small commission on a monthly basis for as long as that person subscribed to that program. This worked out very well. It's quite simple.

Affiliate marketing is a very effective way to make money. Once you have built your email list, you can market to people on an ongoing basis, and as long as you don't overdo it by sending them too many offers, some of those people will stay on your list for years.

The trick with affiliate marketing is to combine it with giving value to the customer via good content. You give first, and then people will reciprocate.

Here's how to create a rapid increase in your income by using the affiliate marketing model:

- Create an email list by giving away a free report (often called a lead magnet) in exchange for their email address.

- Market to your list of prospects your affiliate products in between giving them daily emails of value. Value could be from your blog posts or give them some cool video tips.

- Become proficient at affiliate marketing and email marketing and then create your own course on it. Sell these courses to your list.

- Create books, sell these on Amazon, create audiobooks, sell these on Audible. Link these products back to your lead magnet, your courses, and your website if you have one.

- You can then go one step further and do one-on-one coaching or group coaching on Zoom.

I think you see my point here. Any business can be made even more profitable by just creating better strategies. No matter what business you are in, you can add other levels of income to it by being more creative.

Even the great British pub industry had to change. This is one of our oldest and much-loved industries, but even this had to be dragged, kicking, and screaming into the 21st century.

Pubs In The UK. Then and Now

If you live in the UK or you have visited our country in the past, back in the day, the good old British pub used to do extremely well. There were thousands of them up and down the country.

In 2006, the UK Parliament introduced a smoking ban on all indoor venues. This was a huge blow to the British pub trade. It had always been a tradition to go to the pub for a smoke and a pint.

Many people were now staying at home, drinking cheap supermarket beer whilst puffing away on their cigarettes. This decimated the pub trade.

A lot of the pubs were forced to close and many of them have since been converted into either McDonald's burger restaurants or supermarkets. The pubs that survived were mainly the ones that had been serving meals.

You may well ask, why didn't more pubs serve food in the first place? This could be for a number of reasons, including lack of space, etc. But most of the pubs that went ahead and added another stream of income (food), survived.

People demand more nowadays. In business, you always have to be on the lookout for new trends and be prepared to change to meet the expectations of your market. You have to change things up a bit now and again, offer new products and services.

With pubs, it's beer, food, and football. Pubs have to try and keep people in the pub for longer periods. This way, customers spend more money.

You too also have to keep people in your online business buying for longer. You have to build a following of raving fans. Keep people happy and they will keep coming back for more.

A one-off sale is nice but you don't want your customer buying just one widget and then never seeing them again.

This is where I introduce you to the residual income model

The membership model.

This model works well with or without an actual membership site. "Whaaat?" I hear you say. "No website? How is that even possible?"

Email or Facebook groups.

The membership model can be a paid program delivered either through email, or it can be delivered through a paid

Facebook group. Of course, you can also deliver your paid content through an actual membership site if you wish.

My very first membership model was a paid horse racing handicapping service. Each day, I would deliver horse racing tips to people via email. Not all the horses won of course but people made a profit overall.

I ran this business as a side hustle. It took up very little of my time, but I did let it go after around nine or ten months due to other commitments. It wasn't making a fortune, but it was a nice little income stream, I made around £7000 ($9600) in 10 months.

Membership sites are a great way of generating recurring income, it's not passive income per se, as you do have to be constantly updating the content, but it does work well as a way of bringing in monthly revenue.

For example: Dollar Shave Club

https://dollarshaveclub.com

The Dollar Shave Club provides products for every part of the body you can shave. You purchase razor blades at a monthly subscription price of $9, postage free. You can also buy additional products from their huge range, such as shave butter, pre scrub, hair pomade, and dehydrating shampoo.

This all adds up to a very lucrative business. Dollar Shave Club has around four million members, each paying $9 a month, so their gross monthly turnover just on the monthly blades alone is $36 million dollars.

No wonder Unilever bought the company for a cool 1 billion dollars.

This is just one extreme example. Lots of companies operate on a subscription model. Amazon and Netflix are probably two of the most well-known.

You have a list of customers who pay you a set fee each month for a product or service. You then offer them additional products and services, these are sometimes referred to as upsells.

This keeps everyone happy: your customers get to see and buy your new products, and your business has the benefit of keeping the existing customers all in one place. This opens up the floodgates to keep providing them with even more value and products.

I think you are beginning to see that each and every business can be made into a million-dollar business by adding different models of doing business to the existing model.

Before I really knew this, I used to start a business up and sell products in just one way. This is how many businesses operate today, purely one-dimensional, even though we have this wonderful world of the Internet to reach more customers.

There are no limits to what you can do today. Never in the history of time has there been a better time to start a business. The Internet has opened up a pandora's box of opportunity.

During the recent pandemic, many businesses were caught with their pants down. They believed that the flow of customers buying from them would always be there. Then Covid came along and changed the world.

Who survived relatively unscathed?

1. **Supermarkets and local food stores**
2. **Online stores**

Nearly everyone else encountered problems. Many businesses closed, never to reopen again. Some shops managed to survive: food takeaways did ok, so did stores selling bicycles and health-related products.

The Covid experience has been a huge lesson to many entrepreneurs. In my view, whatever business you are currently running, make sure that you have an internet-based platform to sell products directly to your customers. If you don't, you could be in trouble when the next pandemic hits.

More and more people shop online now and the look of the high street is definitely changing.

This pandemic may have been a hundred-to-one shot, but who knows? We could have another one in a few years' time, or maybe even next year. You can't predict the future, but you can be prepared.

Key takeaways:

• **Multiple streams of income are pretty much essential** – The more passive they are, the better. You can get a lot more done if you have income streams virtually running themselves in the background. As you and your business become more and more successful, you can outsource a lot of the grunt work and have more free time for yourself and your family.

• **Self Publishing, Print on Demand, and Affiliate Marketing** are three great examples of good solid, high demand online businesses. Affiliate marketing is the easiest to set up and has very low start-up costs.

• **The Membership Site subscription model** – We talked about the benefits of having a host of raving fans booked into your membership site paying you a monthly subscription each month. Who doesn't love residual income?

13
KEEP IT SIMPLE

"There are no shortcuts to any place worth going" – *Beverly Sills*

Have you ever been to a Pizza Hut restaurant for a pizza buffet and as you scoop half a ton of pizza slices onto your plate, you spot the ice cream machine out of the corner of your eye?

We have so many choices in life. Sometimes it's best to stick with few choices and focus on those that really matter. Life can get complicated, but business should be simple.

We live in an age where people scroll through everything. People want answers and they want them quickly.

I'm sure everyone has been on a webinar or a Zoom call at some time or other where the host has spent the first twenty minutes talking about himself. In three words. Keep it simple. Don't make it more complicated than it need be.

Find a hungry crowd (demand)

Find a product to serve that crowd

Find a way to get your product to that crowd

Expand your business by adding different income streams

Grow your business by reinvesting the profits

Make your million and enjoy life to the full.

Let's have a recap on what you've learnt in this book. For the first part, we worked on your mind.

Step 1. Fix your brain. I know, this sounds very rude but most of us need a good kick up the ass when it comes to thinking. We tend to look for shortcuts all the time.

When reading a book we often skim through it like a hot knife through butter and wonder why our brain lags behind when it comes to gaining knowledge. Let what you learn stick to your brain.

Always be working on gaining new knowledge.

The five key things to develop for your mind are:

- Developing Lazer Beam Focus

- Dynamic Decision-Making

- How To Develop Bulletproof Resilience

- The Power of Confidence

- The Power of Persistence

From here, we talked about upgrading your peer group. This is so important. The idea here is to always have people who think like you and act like you in your life. Not all of my friends are super positive or supportive, but some are.

Maybe you just like having people around; there should always be a reason why you have someone in your life.

Perhaps they encourage you, maybe they make you smile, or maybe they just listen to all your rubbish. We all need good friends. But, we also need to be around people who inspire us and who are also on the same journey as us.

Life as an entrepreneur can be a very lonely life. Most people don't or won't understand us. We are pretty much in this by ourselves. That's why every now and again, we need to be around those people who inspire us and are moving in the same direction as we are.

There are plenty of meet-up groups in and around your area, or you can arrange your own meet-ups through social media. I'm sure there are lots of like minded people in your area. people who are on the same journey as you.

We then stepped into the practical side. It's OK knowing what to do but we also need to know how.

Step 2. Choose Your Business.

Choose wisely. There are so many business opportunities out there, it's a wonder that anyone stays in any one business for any length of time. It's like that pizza buffet we talked about earlier. There are so many shiny objects out there each day to distract us.

The truth is, most of today's shiny objects end up being yesterday's stale bread. Although some of these opportunities occasionally shine and last for a while, most disappear without a trace, leaving a lot of people out of pocket.

My advice here is to stick to the fundamentals. Don't build a business out of smoke and mirrors. People want and will always want good products that solve their problems. Offer solutions not #BS.

I wrote this book to solve people's problems.

When you are a problem solver, people will come back to you time and time again.

Build your business on a solid foundation. Give people what they want, not just what YOU want. When you are deciding on which business to go into, decide on a business that you will enjoy doing for the next few years.

Don't start something that you'll get fed up with in a few months time. Enthusiasm goes a long way in business.

Be realistic.

Start your business, open a business bank account, and put in your starting capital. Keep a separate amount of money in another account just in case you need more capital in a few months down the line.

Decide on the method of distribution.

Which modality are you going to use to distribute your products or service? Are you going to sell via an eCom site, are you going to use Facebook and Facebook ads. Or maybe you are going to use eBay or Etsy?

Get all of these things sorted out before you start. Don't wait until the day you start your business to decide where and when you will sell your products. Plan everything in advance.

Keep a journal each day specifically for your business. Plan each day, the evening before. Wake up early, get some work in before you go off to your job, if you are employed.

Always keep reminding yourself of your 'Why'.

There will be times when you are fed up and you may even think of quitting. Don't do it. Remind yourself of why you started in the first place.

Is it for your family? Or are you sick and tired of working for a boss? Are you fed up always struggling with money and continuously having to check prices before buying?

If your why is big enough you will make it to the finish line. You can't stop someone who won't be stopped. He or she will always find a way through in the end.

The Power of Problems.

This actually comes under the heading of 'keeping it realistic' but I'll go over it here. You will never have a life free of problems. It's impossible. But, you can always learn from each and every one of them.

Just like the day I lost $250,000 in one day. I learned from it. I had to. I won't do that again. Without problems, there is no hope. This might sound like a crazy thing to say, but it's true.

Problems are our greatest teachers.

If everything worked out well all the time we would never learn anything, we would take things for granted, and people too. Problems keep us on our toes and give us a wonderful learning experience.

Think of a problem as a lesson.

Problems actually make people stronger.

When you start to see problems for what they really are and not the minefields that people think they are, you are starting to make progress, you are beginning to make yourself 'bulletproof'.

Being bulletproof will mean that problems will just bounce off you like a superhero. It's not what happens to you that coins, it's how you react to what happens.

Key takeaways:

- **Keep on track** - Don't get distracted by shiny objects. Today's "next big thing" often becomes yesterday's stale bread. Don't buy into the hype. It's usually #BS

- **The Power of Problems** - Problems can actually be good for you. They can keep you from getting too complacent and are wonderful life lessons.

See you in our final chapter.

14
ADVICE FROM THE HEART

The first thing I would like to say to you is congratulations on getting this far in the book. You might find this hard to believe but when people buy self-help books, around 60% of them don't even get past the first chapter.

Some don't even open the book.

I know this sounds crazy, but many people want to achieve a lot, but give very little. There are so many shiny objects out there, people often end up collecting books they never read and collecting apps and programs they do nothing with.

Inertia kills a lot of people's dreams stone dead.

This chapter is pure advice from the heart. I'm not teaching anything here. I'm hopefully passing on some valuable wisdom that I have learnt over the years. Let's face it, we all need inspiration.

Let's go. Have a read of these every day for inspiration.

#1. **If you never go after it, you'll never get it**. Life shouldn't be about the things 'we didn't do'. It should be a storybook of things that we did do. Imagine that your life is a movie: would you pay to go and see it? You are defined by the things that you do, not by the things that you thought about doing.

#2. **Don't spend your life worrying about the past or what might happen in the future**. The past has gone, let it go. Whatever happened, forgive, forget and move on. The future isn't here yet, it's up to you to create it today, but stop worrying about it. Worry is the interest paid in advance on things that rarely happen.

#3. **Keep smiling**. Don't let the world upset you. When you smile, your brain releases tiny molecules called neuropeptides. These help fight off stress. You also release endorphins which can act as a mild pain reliever and dopamine which can help you to feel happy.

All this from just a smile. If that's what a smile can do for you, imagine what you are doing to others by smiling. Smiling is contagious. The universe rewards those who share love and kindness.

#4. **On your way up, never lose sight of the people you knew before you were successful.** You might meet them on the way down. Give respect to everyone in the same way that you yourself would want to be respected.

#5. **Make others feel good.** Always leave other people feeling like they've won. Try to make every transaction and interaction that you have with others a win/win situation for both of you. This way, you will never be short of people who support you.

#6. **You can't get a little bit pregnant**. Commit to things, and see them through. You'll never make much progress in life if you keep quitting. Be the example, say you will do something, do it. This is the mark of a leader.

#7. **It's never too late to start over**. There are no rules about starting a new life. If you think you're too old, you're already defeated. People start new lives, new hobbies, new businesses, new sports and new adventures well into their 80s, 90s, and even into their 100s.

Don't wait around waiting for death, it's going to come to us all whether we like it or not. You can spend the rest of your life doing nothing but waiting, or you can spend it making a difference. Go out with a BANG!

#8. **Respect people, but don't put them on a pedestal**. Admiring people and their achievements is fine but don't make people out to be gods. Even Kings and Queens use the toilet on occasion. Admire people but don't think that they are any better than you.

#9. **Not everyone will fit your pictures**. Don't punish people for not being who you want them to be. I know this is frustrating, but people are not robots, they were not born to serve you or conform to your views of the world.

We all have our strange, funny ways. People will often disappoint you, especially if your expectations of them is set too high. Learn to live with people's faults and your life will be a lot less frustrating and a lot happier.

#10. **Be bold.** No one ever made their mark on this world by watching someone else get all the glory. In order to get what you want, you have to get your face out there, be counted and stop being afraid. I see people wishing for things all the time, but doing very little to get them.

#11. **Be grateful, be thankful**. Long-term happiness will never be found in just having material things. Be grateful for just being alive. You are probably better off than most people in this world. Keep your chin up every day and live life to be happy. Despite what some people say, happiness is not fleeting, it's permanent. You are about as happy as you decide to be.

#12. **Don't let people tell you, you can't do it.** If another human being has already done it, it is almost certain that you can too. Not everyone will have your interests at heart. They are too busy running their own life. You will also find that some people although on the surface, they want you to win, underneath, they secretly want you to fail. The best advice here is, follow your heart.

#13. **You can't eliminate bad days.** However, you can change your attitude toward them. The universe will try to balance your bad and good days out over time. Unfortunately, just like buses here in the UK, bad days often cluster together. Treat every bad day as a test.

You can't have a life free of challenges, you can only improve the way that you react to them. After reading this book, you should now be well on your way to achieving this.

Please promise me two things:

1) **You will practice everything in this book** and create something amazing for yourself and your family. I'm sure that you won't want to stop at the magic million. Why not go on, blaze a trail and build a 10, 20, or even 100 million dollar business empire?

2) **If you got a lot of value from this book**, please leave me an honest review on Amazon, or wherever you bought this book.

Getting reviews helps this book to be seen by more people, and helps me to produce even more good books to inspire and help other people along on their journey.

It's been an absolute pleasure. Let's do this again sometime.

CONCLUSION

The Pareto Principle

I want you to go back to 1923 for a moment. A great man died in that year called Vilfredo Pareto. You may not have heard of him but he was the founder of the Pareto Principle. This is often known as the 80/20 principle.

The Pareto Principle states that **80% of consequences come from 20% of the causes**. This principle, which was derived from the imbalance of land ownership in Italy, is commonly used to illustrate the notion that not all things are equal, and that the minority owns the majority.

It's quite common knowledge that a small percentage of people in this world own most of the world's wealth.

This principle is one of the most powerful pieces of information I've ever come across, and can easily be funnelled into your life and your business once you understand it.

Around 20% of all that you do will be responsible for around 80% of your results. This isn't an exact science of course, but the principle itself is pretty accurate.

What does this mean for us?

Don't ever just write one book. If you write ten books, two of them (20%) will probably get you 80% of the results .

When starting a business, increase your modalities and the product range itself over time as 20% of your methods and products will get you 80% of your results. This means that 80% of what you do will only get you 20% of the results.

Doesn't it make sense to put more time and effort into the 20% of things that give you 80% of the results?

When making new friends, don't just go out and make one. Make ten, as two of those friends will equal 80% of your best experiences.

I think you get the picture.

You now have all the keys that you will ever need to start your very own multi-million dollar business. What will you do next?.

Remember earlier when I said that some people don't even get past the first chapter when they buy a book?. Well, you've finally got here. That says a lot about you.

However, now you need to take action on starting your business. Don't be one of those professional book readers who read tons of self-help books but never do anything with the information.

I have made and lost a lot of money in my life. The best times have always followed the hardest of times. You can't make yourself a king's ransom sitting still and not taking action.

Now is the time to go out there and show everyone you can do it. Being an entrepreneur can be a great life. There is something very attractive about running your own show.

Remember this quote: write it down and keep it with you:

> "Entrepreneurship is living a few years of your life like most people won't. So that you can spend the rest of your life like most people can't". - Unknown

If you want a million dollars, you have to do things that most people won't. This could mean getting up early and working on your business before you go to your job. It could mean working on the weekend or holidays. Whatever it means, it's worth it.

Life is meant to be a growth centric experience. Let's face it, if you're not loving your life, you won't be too keen on death either. You owe it to yourself, and family to shoot for the best you can be.

I would rather spend just one year as millionaire, than a whole lifetime wondering what it would be like to be one. **You were born to be great**. You can spend your whole life wishing things would happen, you can spend your whole life watching others make it happen. Better still, you could spend your whole life making it happen. Take action, go out and grab life by the danglies. **Don't ever give up.**

If you loved this book..

Please do leave an honest review for me over at Amazon. Reviews are the lifeblood of a book, especially in the early days. More reviews = more readers, and that helps me create more books for you.

And last but not least. I have a great free gift waiting for you over at. https://keitheverett.co.uk/freeforyou

SOURCES AND RESOURCES

Join me on Facebook. I have a free private group on there called 'Inspired To Make Money'. https://keitheverett.co.uk/facebook

Grab a FREE copy of Millionaire Shortcuts

https://keitheverett.co.uk/freeforyou

My Blog: https://keitheverett.co.uk

Other books from this author

Money Mind Crush. This is a book on how to develop that winning mindset to attract all the money that you could possibly want.

Awesome Kindle Book Ideas. This is a book on how to find a flood of ideas for your non-fiction Kindle books.

How To Write A Book. This book is all about how to create your own non-fiction book. It covers just about everything you need to know on how to write a book and get it ready for self-publishing.

Other recommended books:

Love Yourself Deeply – Rebecca Collins. This book is about self-love for women. Learn to love yourself deeply, glow with self-confidence and get your self-esteem back.

Sources

Stone, Oliver. 1987. Wall Street. United States: Twentieth Century Fox

Pytka, Joe. 1989. Let It Ride. United States: Paramount Pictures

Lucasfilm Ltd.; 2013. Star Wars Original Trilogy. United States. Twentieth Century Fox Home Entertainment

Mischel, W., & Ebbesen, E. B. (1970). Attention in delay of gratification. Journal of Personality and Social Psychology, 16(2), 329.

Global Wealth Report, 2021, Credit Suisse Research Institute

https://www.credit-suisse.com/about-us/en/reports-research/global-wealth-report.html

https://www.weforum.org/agenda/2021/06/remote-workers-burnout-covid-microsoft-survey/

Hill, Napoleon, 2005, Think And Grow Rich, Tarcher Perigee Publishers

Durham City Incubator, 2019

https://dcincubator.co.uk/blog/60-of-new-businesses-fail-in-the-first-3-years-heres-why/

Stanford university marshmallow experiment of 1972

https://bingschool.stanford.edu/news/bing-marshmallow-studies-50-years-continuing-research

Wim Hoff Breathing method

https://www.wimhofmethod.com/practice-the-method

Gig Broking Method: https://keitheverett.co.uk/how-to-make-money-from-home-as-a-gig-broker/

www.ingramcontent.com/pod-product-compliance
Lightning Source LLC
Chambersburg PA
CBHW071520080526
44588CB00011B/1502